PRESENTED TO

Christmas
Stories for the
Heart

(*Keepsakes for the Heart* is an elegant gift collection that
includes a hardbound book with full-color artwork,
complementary bookmark, note cards,
and a charming box for keepsakes.)

Christmas Stories for the Heart

COMPILED *by* ALICE GRAY

Multnomah Publishers *Sisters, Oregon*

Christmas Stories for the Heart

Published by Multnomah Gift Books
a division of Multnomah Publishers, Inc.

© 1997, 2000 by Multnomah Publishers, Inc.

International Standard Book Number: 1-57673-845-0

Cover photo by Tony Stone Images

Cover design by The Office of Bill Chiaravalle

Printed in the United States of America

Scripture quotations are from:
The New Living Translation (NLT) © 1996 by Tyndale House Publishers, Inc.
The King James Version (KJV)

00 01 02 03 04 05 06 07— 16 15 14 13 12 11 10 9

In Celebration of —

CHRISTMAS

*Blessed is the season which engages the
whole world in a celebration of love.*

HAMILTON WRIGHT MABIE

CONTENTS

CONTENTS

*C*hristmas seemed so much simpler when I was a child.

The decorations were simple, the gifts were simple, the traditions were simple. There was nothing elaborate, complicated, or pressured about the Christmas season.

In fact, it seemed like pure magic.

I remember the winter chill...the friends and cousins from far away...the decorations on the lampposts downtown...and brightly wrapped gifts piled under the tree. Most of all, I remember our little manger and the story of the Greatest Gift the world has ever known.

Then something changed.

I grew up.

Somehow, in the passing of time, the thrill of those childhood Christmases began to fade. I began to think of Christmas as season of extra demands and stress. The preparations began to seem so complicated, involved, and expensive. That simple joy, that childlike sense of wonder and awe became layered over with commercialism, chaotic schedules, unrealistic expectations—and maybe just a little bit of cynicism.

Christmas wasn't fun anymore. I began to dread December.

And now? I want to go back. I want to rediscover what I lost between those simple, childhood traditions and the holiday chaos of the last few years. I want to focus again on the Truth behind the wonder.

The book you hold in your hands right now can really help. Within these pages, you'll encounter stories that will bring back some of the emotions you thought you'd left behind years ago. The laughter, joy, and even tears in these tenderly chosen stories will help you set aside the holiday pressures for a while—or, better still, help you put them in the right perspective. You'll begin to remember again what the season is all about...and Whom the season is all about.

And you just may find a smile returning to your face, and a twinkle returning to your eye.

Christmas is still a wonder. It always will be. But sometimes we need a little reminding.

CHRISTMAS TREASURES

THE MANGER WAS EMPTY
Retold by Casandra Lindell

He arrived early on Christmas morning to give the church a thorough inspection, noting with approval that the aisles and seats had been swept and dusted after the midnight Christmas Eve service. Any lost purses, Bibles, and gloves had been collected and sent to the office where the lost and found box was kept; every forgotten flyer and bulletin insert had been rounded up and discarded.

Outside it was just beginning to grow light. In the church, where only the pastor moved, candles flickered and threw shifting shadows on the arches and the stone floor. Occasionally, stray candlelight picked out the rich colors in the stained glass windows. It was cold and, except for the pastor's slow tread, it was silent.

He paused beside the almost life-sized nativity scene to say a Christmas prayer of thanksgiving to the One whose birth is celebrated. The figures, each lovingly crafted with wonderful realism, sat on a small stage. A night sky and the star that led the shepherds and the wise men to the Messiah on the day of His birth could be seen through the open door of the stable. The shepherds were just entering, eyes wide in obvious awe. Various kinds of livestock stood in stalls or lay on the edges of the scene. And in the center was the Holy Family. Looking at the manger scene, the pastor could almost feel the reverence of that long-ago night.

Slowly, a puzzled frown crept across his brow. Then his choked gasp rustled through the empty church.

The manger was empty! The small figure representing the infant Savior was gone.

Hurriedly, and with growing agitation, the pastor began to search the church again. Starting by the manger, he peered back through the aisles, nearly crawling on his hands and knees to see all the way under each seat. But there was nothing. Next, he called the custodian, thinking he may have seen the figure of the infant Jesus. Then he called the assistant pastor and all the elders, but no one had any explanation. In the end, each shaking his head sorrowfully, they accepted the truth they had all been trying to avoid: The figure could not have been mislaid or lost—it must have been stolen.

With solemnity befitting the occasion, the pastor reported the theft to the congregation that assembled not long after. His voice trembled as he told them what he had found earlier that morning. For a person to steal the very symbol of their reason for celebrating, he said, their very reason for hope—well, he just did not understand. His gaze swept over the faces in the early morning congregation, disappointed to think someone in his own congregation might do such a thing.

"The figure of the Christ Child," he said, "must be returned before this Christmas Day is over. No one will ask any questions, but it must be brought back immediately." Then, he slipped from the pulpit and the choir closed the service with a Christmas hymn, "O Come, Let Us Adore Him."

The manger remained empty throughout the day.

Toward the end of the afternoon, discouraged and heavy-hearted, the pastor took a walk through the wintry streets of the neighborhood. Ahead of him he saw one of the youngest members of his flock, a six-year-old boy named Tommy. Bundled shabbily against the cold, Tommy trudged up the sidewalk, proudly dragging behind him a toy express wagon. It was bright and red and obviously Christmas-new.

Knowing what sacrifice and scrimping the purchase of this toy must have meant—Tommy's family could barely make ends meet—the pastor was deeply touched. The love Tommy's parents had for their little boy gave the pastor's heart a gentle warmth, and he felt his faith in human nature beginning to return. He sped up so he could wish Tommy a merry Christmas and admire the beautiful new wagon.

But as he drew nearer he saw that the wagon was not empty—there lay the baby Jesus, now wrapped and blanketed but not quite hidden.

The pastor crouched down beside Tommy, one knee feeling the damp snow through his pant leg. His face was grim and disappointed. Tommy may be just a little boy, and one must make allowances of course—but he was still old enough to understand that stealing was very wrong. The pastor made this crystal clear to Tommy while the little boy stood, his seemingly guiltless clear eyes filling with what the pastor was sure were penitent tears.

"But, Pastor," the small boy quavered when at last the man finished talking, "I didn't *steal* Jesus. It wasn't like that at all." He paused to swallow hard and wipe a few tears away. "It's just that I've been asking Him for a red wagon as a Christmas present for a long time—and I promised Him that when I got it I'd take Him out for the first ride."

TROUBLE AT THE INN

Dina Donohue

*W*ally was nine that year and in the second grade, though he should have been in the fourth. Most people in town knew that he had difficulty in keeping up. He was big and clumsy, slow in movement and mind. Still, Wally was well liked by the other children in his class, all of whom were smaller than he, though the boys had trouble hiding their irritation when Wally would ask to play ball with them—or play any game for that matter in which winning was most important.

Most often they would find a way to keep him out, but Wally would hang around anyway—not sulking, just hoping. He was always a helpful boy, a willing and smiling one, and the natural protector, paradoxically, of the underdog. Sometimes if the older boys chased the younger ones away, it would always be Wally who'd say, "Can't they stay? They're no bother."

Wally fancied the idea of being a shepherd with a flute in the Christmas pageant that year, but the play's director, Miss Lumbard, assigned him to a more important role. After all, she reasoned, the Innkeeper did not have too many lines, and Wally's size would make his refusal of lodging to Joseph more forceful.

And so it happened that the usual large audience gathered for the town's yearly extravaganza of crèches, beards, crowns, halos and a whole stage full of squeaky voices. No one on stage or off was more caught up in the magic of the night than Wallace Purling. They said later that he stood in the wings and watched the performance with such fascination that from time to time Miss Lumbard had to make sure he didn't wander onstage before his cue.

Then the time came when Joseph appeared, slowly, tenderly guiding Mary to the door of the inn. Joseph knocked hard on the wooden door set into the painted backdrop. Wally the Innkeeper was there, waiting.

"What do you want?" demanded Wally, swinging the door open with a brusque gesture.

"We seek lodging."

"Seek it elsewhere." Wally looked straight ahead but spoke vigorously. "The inn is filled."

"Sir, we have asked everywhere in vain. We have traveled far and are very weary."

"There is no room in this inn for you." Wally looked properly stern.

"Please, good innkeeper, this is my wife, Mary. She is heavy with child and needs a place to rest. Surely you must have some small corner for her. She is so tired."

Now, for the first time, the Innkeeper relaxed his stiff stance and looked down at Mary. With that, there was a long pause, long enough to make the audience a bit tense with embarrassment.

"No! Be gone!" the prompter whispered from the wings.

"No!" Wally repeated automatically. "Be gone!"

Joseph placed his arm around Mary and Mary laid her head upon her husband's shoulder and the two of them started to move away. The Innkeeper did not return inside his inn, however. Wally stood there in the doorway, watching the forlorn couple. His mouth was open, his brow creased with concern, his eyes filling unmistakably with tears.

And suddenly this Christmas pageant became different from all others.

"Don't go, Joseph," Wally called out. "Bring Mary back." And Wallace Purling's face grew into a bright smile. "You can have my room."

THE GOLD AND IVORY TABLECLOTH
Howard C. Schade

REPRINTED WITH PERMISSION FROM THE
DECEMBER 1954 *READER'S DIGEST*

At Christmastime men and women everywhere gather in their churches to wonder anew at the greatest miracle the world has ever known. But the story I like best to recall was not a miracle—not exactly.

It happened to a pastor who was very young. His church was very old. Once, long ago, it had flourished. Famous men had preached from its pulpit, prayed before its altar. Rich and poor alike worshipped there and built it beautifully. Now the good days had passed from the section of town where it stood. But the pastor and his young wife believed in their run-down church. They felt that with paint, hammer, and faith they could get it in shape. Together they went to work.

But in late December a severe storm whipped through the river valley, and the worst blow fell on the little church—a huge chunk of rain-soaked plaster fell out of the inside wall just behind the altar. Sorrowfully, the pastor and his wife swept away the mess, but they couldn't hide the ragged hole.

The pastor looked at it and had to remind himself quickly, "Thy will be done!" But his wife wept, "Christmas is only two days away!"

That afternoon the dispirited couple attended the auction held for the benefit of a youth group. The auctioneer opened a box and shook out of its folds a handsome gold-and-ivory lace tablecloth. It was a magnificent item, nearly fifteen feet long. But it, too, dated from a long-vanished era. Who, today, had any use for such a thing? There were a few halfhearted bids. Then the pastor was seized with what he thought was a great idea. He bid it in for $6.50.

He carried the cloth back to the church and tacked it up on the wall behind the altar. It completely hid the hole! And the extraordinary beauty of its shimmering handwork cast a fine, holiday glow over the chancel. It was a great triumph. Happily he went back to preparing his Christmas sermon.

Just before noon on the day of Christmas Eve, as the pastor was opening the church, he noticed a woman standing in the cold at the bus stop.

"The bus won't be here for forty minutes!" he called, and invited her into the church to get warm.

She told him that she had come from the city that morning to be interviewed for a job as governess to the children of one of the wealthy families in town but she had been turned down. A war refugee, her English was imperfect.

The woman sat down in a pew and chafed her hands and rested. After a while she dropped her head and prayed. She looked up as the pastor began to adjust the great ivory-and-gold lace cloth across the hole. She rose suddenly and walked up the steps of the chancel. She looked at the tablecloth. The pastor smiled and started to tell her about the storm damage, but she didn't seem to listen. She took up a fold of the cloth and rubbed it between her fingers.

"It is mine!" she said. "It is my banquet cloth!" She lifted the corner and showed the surprised pastor that there were initials monogrammed on it. "My husband had the cloth made especially for me in Brussels! There could not be another like it."

For the next few minutes the woman and the pastor talked excitedly together. She explained that she was Viennese; that she and her husband had opposed the Nazis and decided to leave the country. They were advised to go separately. Her husband put her on a train for Switzerland. They planned that he would join her as soon as he could arrange to ship their household goods across the border.

She never saw him again. Later she heard that he had died in a concentration camp.

"I have always felt that it was my fault—to leave without him," she said. "Perhaps these years of wandering have been my punishment!"

The pastor tried to comfort her and urged her to take the cloth with her. She refused. Then she went away.

As the church began to fill on Christmas Eve, it was clear that the cloth was going to be a great success. It had been skillfully designed to look its best by candlelight.

After the service, the pastor stood in the doorway; many people told him that the church looked beautiful. One gentle-faced, middle-aged man—he was the local clock-and-watch repairman—looked rather puzzled.

"It is strange," he said in his soft accent. "Many years ago my wife—God rest her—and I owned such a cloth. In our home in Vienna, my wife put it on the table—" here he smiled—"only when the bishop came to dinner!"

The pastor suddenly became very excited. He told the jeweler about the woman who had been in the church earlier in the day.

The startled jeweler clutched the pastor's arm. "Can it be? Does she live?"

Together the two got in touch with the family who had interviewed her. Then, in the pastor's car they started for the city. And as Christmas

Day was born, this man and his wife—who had been separated through so many saddened Yuletides—were reunited.

To all who heard this story, the joyful purpose of the storm that knocked a hole in the wall of the church was now quite clear. Of course, people said it was a miracle, and I think you will agree it was the season for it!

IF YOU'RE MISSING
BABY JESUS, CALL 7162
Jean Gietzen

W hen I was a child, my father worked for an oil company in North Dakota. The company moved him around to different parts of the state and at some point between one move and another, we lost our family nativity set. Shortly before Christmas in 1943, my mother decided to replace it and was happy to find another at our local five and dime for only $3.99. When my brother Tom and I helped her unpack the set, we discovered two figures of the Baby Jesus.

"Someone must have packaged this wrong," my mother said, counting out the figures. "We have one Joseph, one Mary, three wise men, three shepherds, two lambs, a donkey, a cow, an angel, and two babies. Oh, dear! I suppose some set down at the store is missing a Baby Jesus."

"Hey, that's great, Mom," my brother and I shouted. "Now we have twins!"

"You two run back down to the store and tell the manager that we have an extra Jesus. Tell him to put a sign on the remaining boxes saying that if a set is missing a Baby Jesus, call 7162," my mother instructed. "I'll give each of you a penny for some candy. And don't forget your mufflers. It's freezing cold out there."

The manager of the store copied down my mother's message and the next time we were in the store we saw the cardboard sign that read, "If you're missing Baby Jesus, call 7162."

All week long we waited for the call to come. Surely, we thought, someone was missing the important figurine. Each time the phone rang, my mother would say, "I'll bet that's about Jesus," but it never was. My father tried to explain that the figurine could be missing from a set in Walla Walla, Washington, and that packing errors occurred all the time. He suggested we just put the extra Jesus back in the box and forget about it.

"Back in the box!" I wailed. "What a terrible thing to do to the Baby Jesus. And at Christmastime, too."

"Surely someone will call," my mother said. "We'll just keep them together in the manger until someone calls."

When no call had come by 5:00 on Christmas Eve, my mother insisted that my father "just run down to the store" to see if there were any sets left. "You can see them right through the window, over on the counter," she said. "If they are all gone, I'll know someone is bound to call tonight."

"Run down to the store?" my father thundered. "It's fifteen degrees below zero out there!"

"Oh, Daddy, we'll go with you," I said. "Tommy and I will bundle up good. And we can look at all the decorations on the way."

My father gave a long sigh and headed for the front closet. "I can't believe I'm doing this," he muttered. "Each time the phone rings everyone yells at me to see if it's about Jesus, and now I'm going off on the coldest night of the year to peek in a window to see if He's there or not there."

My father muttered all the way down the block while my brother and I raced each other up to the window where the tiny lights flickered on and off around the frame. "They're all gone, Daddy," I shouted. "Every set must be sold."

"Hooray, hooray!" my brother joined in, catching up with me. "The mystery will be solved tonight!"

My father, who had remained several steps behind us, turned on his heel and headed back home.

Inside the house once more, we saw that the extra figurine had vanished from the set and my mother appeared to have vanished, too. "Someone must have called and she went out to deliver the figurine," my father reasoned, pulling off his boots. "You kids get busy stringing popcorn strands for the tree and I'll wrap your mother's present."

We had almost completed one strand when the phone rang. My father yelled for me to answer it. "Tell 'em we found a home for Jesus," he called down the steps. But the caller was not an inquirer. It was my mother with instructions for us to come to 205 Chestnut Street immediately and bring three blankets, a box of cookies, and some milk.

"Now what has she gotten us into?" my father groaned as we bundled up again. "205 Chestnut Street. Why, that's about eight blocks away. Wrap that milk up good in the blankets or it will turn to ice by the time we get there. Why in the name of heaven can't we all just get on with Christmas? It's probably twenty degrees below out there now. And the wind is picking up. Of all the crazy things to do on a night like this."

Tommy and I sang Christmas songs at the top of our lungs all the way to Chestnut Street. My father, carrying his bundle of blankets and milk, looked for all the world like St. Nicholas himself with his arms full of goodies. Every now and then my brother would call back to him, "Let's pretend we're looking for a place to stay, Dad, just like Joseph and Mary."

"Let's pretend we are in Bethlehem where it is probably sixty-five degrees in the shade right now," my father would answer.

The house at 205 Chestnut Street turned out to be the darkest one on the block. One tiny light burned in the living room and the moment we set foot on the porch steps, my mother opened the door and shouted,

"They're here, they're here. Oh, thank God you got here, Ray! You kids take those blankets into the living room and wrap up the little ones on the couch. I'll take the milk and cookies."

"Would you mind telling me what is going on, Ethel?" my father asked. "We have just walked through below zero weather with the wind in our faces all the way...."

"Never mind all that now," my mother interrupted. "There is no heat in this house and this young mother is so upset she doesn't know what to do. Her husband walked out on her and those poor children will have to spend a very bleak Christmas, so don't you complain. I told her you could fix that oil furnace in a jiffy."

My mother strode off to the kitchen to warm the milk while my brother and I wrapped up the five little children who were huddled together on the couch. The children's mother explained to my father that her husband had run off, taking bedding, clothing, and almost every piece of furniture, but she had been doing all right until the furnace broke down.

"I been doin' washin' and ironin' for people and cleanin' the five and dime," she said. "I saw your number every day there, on those boxes on the counter. When the furnace went out, that number kept goin' through my mind: 7162. 7162.

"Said on the box that if a person was missin' Jesus, they should call you. That's how I knew you were good Christian people, willin' to help folks. I figured that maybe you would help me, too. So I stopped at the grocery store tonight and I called your missus. I'm not missin' Jesus, mister, because I sure love the Lord. But I am missin' heat.

"Me and the kids ain't got no beddin', no warm clothes. I got a few Christmas toys for them, but I got no money to fix that furnace."

"Okay, okay," my father said kindly. "You've come to the right place. Now let's see. You've got a little oil burner over there in the dining room. Shouldn't be too hard to fix. Probably just a clogged flue. I'll look it over, see what it needs."

My mother came into the living room carrying a plate of cookies and a tray with warm milk. As she set the cups down on the coffee table, I noticed the figure of the Baby Jesus lying in the center of the table. It was the only sign of the Christmas season in the house. The children stared wide-eyed with wonder at the plate of cookies my mother set before them. One of the littlest ones woke up and crawled out from under the blanket. Seeing all the strangers in his house, he began to cry. My mother swooped him up in her arms and began to sing to him.

"This, this, is Christ the King, Whom shepherds guard and angels sing," she crooned while the child wailed. "Haste, haste to bring Him laud, the Babe, the son of Mary," she sang, oblivious to the child's cries. She sang and danced the baby around the room until he settled down again.

"You hear that, Chester?" the young mother said to another child. "That woman is singin' 'bout the Lord Jesus. He ain't ever gonna walk out on us. Why, He sent these people to us just to fix our furnace. And blankets we got now, too. Oh, we'll be warm tonight."

My father, finishing his work on the oil burner, wiped his hands on his muffler and said, "I've got it going, but you need more oil. I'll make a few calls tonight when I get home and we'll get you some oil. Yessir, you came to the right place," he grinned.

When my father calculated that the furnace was going strong once more, our family bundled up and made our way home. My father didn't say a thing about the cold weather and had barely set foot inside the front door when he was on the phone.

"Ed, hey, how are ya, Ed?" I heard him say. "Yes, Merry Christmas to you, too. Say Ed, we have kind of an unusual situation here and I know you've got that pickup truck. I wonder if we could round up some of the boys and find a Christmas tree, you know, and a couple of things for..."

The rest of his conversation was lost in a blur of words as my brother and I ran to our rooms and began pulling clothes out of our closets and toys off of our shelves. My mother checked through our belongings for sizes and games she said "might do" and added some of her own sweaters and slacks to our stack. We were up way past our bedtime that night wrapping our gifts. The men my father had called found oil for the furnace, bedding, two chairs, three lamps and had made two trips to 205 Chestnut before the night was done. Our gifts were piled into the truck on the second trip, and even though it must have been thirty degrees below by then, my father let us ride along in the back of the truck.

No one ever did call about the missing figurine in the nativity set, but as I grow older I realize that it wasn't a packing mistake at all.

A BIT OF ETERNITY
Author unknown

*Y*ears ago in England there was a postal clerk whose job it was to sort through the mail and separate all of the Christmas letters addressed to Santa Claus. One day he came across an envelope with his own return address, and he recognized his little daughter's handwriting. He opened it and found the words she had written:

Dear Santa Claus,

We are very sad at our home this year. Little Charlie, my brother, went up to heaven last week and when you come to my house can you get his toys and take them to him? I'll leave them in the corner by the chimney—his hobbyhorse, his train, and everything. You see he might miss them in heaven. . .especially his horse. He loved riding that horse so much. So just take them to him and you don't need to give anything to me. But if you could leave something for my Daddy that will make him stop crying, it would be the best thing you could do for me. I heard him tell Mommy that only eternity could cure him. Could you give him some of that?

Were earth a thousand times as fair,

Beset with gold and jewels rare,

She yet were far too poor to be

A narrow cradle, Lord, for Thee.

Martin Luther

HI THERE!

Nancy Dahlberg

t was Sunday, Christmas. Our family had spent the holidays in San
Francisco with my husband's parents. But in order for us to be back
at work on Monday, we found ourselves driving the 400 miles back home
to Los Angeles on Christmas Day.

We stopped for lunch in King City. The restaurant was nearly empty.
We were the only family and ours were the only children. I heard Erik, my
one-year-old, squeal with glee: "Hi there. Hi there." He pounded his fat baby
hands—whack, whack—on the metal highchair tray. His face was alive with
excitement, eyes wide, gums bared in a toothless grin. He wriggled, and
chirped, and giggled, and then I saw the source of his merriment. . .and my
eyes could not take it all in at once.

A tattered rag of a coat obviously bought by someone else eons ago—
dirty, greasy, and worn. . .baggy pants—spindly body—toes that poked out
of would-be shoes. . .a shirt that had ring-around-the-color all over, and a
face like none other. . .gums as bare as Erik's.

"Hi there, baby; hi there, big boy. I see ya, buster."

My husband and I exchanged a look that was a cross between "What
do we do?" and "Poor devil."

Our meal came, and the cacophony continued. Now the old bum was
shouting from across the room: "Do ya know patty cake? Atta boy. . .Do ya
know peek-a-boo? Hey, look he knows peek-a-boo!"

Erik continued to laugh and answer, "Hi there." Every call was echoed.
Nobody thought it was cute. The guy was a drunk and a disturbance. I was
embarrassed. My husband, Dennis, was humiliated. Even our six-year-old

said, "Why is that old man talking so loud?"

Dennis went to pay the check, imploring me to get Erik and meet him in the parking lot. "Lord, just let me out of here before he speaks to me or Erik." I bolted for the door.

It soon was obvious that both the Lord and Erik had other plans. As I drew closer to the man, I turned my back, walking to sidestep him—and any air he might be breathing. As I did so, Erik, with his eyes riveted on his new friend, leaned far over my arm, reaching with both his hands in a baby's "pick me up" position.

In a split second of balancing my baby and turning to counter his weight, I came eye to eye with the old man. Erik was lunging for him, arms spread wide.

The bum's eyes both asked and implored, "Would you let me hold your baby?"

There was no need for me to answer because Erik propelled himself from my arms into the man's. Suddenly a very old man and very young baby consummated their love relationship. Erik laid his tiny head upon the man's ragged shoulder. The man's eyes closed, and I saw tears hover beneath his lashes. His aged hands full of grime, and pain, and hard labor—gently, so gently, cradled my baby's bottom and stroked his back.

I stood awestruck. The old man rocked and cradled Erik in his arms for a moment, and then his eyes opened and set squarely on mine. He said in a firm commanding voice, "You take care of this baby."

Somehow I managed, "I will," from a throat that contained a stone.

He pried Erik from his chest—unwillingly, longingly— as though he were in pain.

I held my arms open to receive my baby and again the gentleman addressed me.

"God bless you, ma'am. You've given me my Christmas gift."

I said nothing more than a muttered thanks.

With Erik back in my arms, I ran for the car. Dennis wondered why I was crying and holding Erik so tightly and why I was saying, "My God, my God, forgive me."

A STRING OF BLUE BEADS

Fulton Oursler

*P*ete Richards was the loneliest man in town on the day Jean Grace opened his door. You may have seen something in the newspapers about the incident at the time it happened, although neither his name nor hers was published, nor was the full story told as I tell it here.

Pete's shop had come down to him from his grandfather. The little front window was strewn with a disarray of old-fashioned things: bracelets and lockets worn in days before the Civil War, gold rings and silver boxes, images of jade and ivory, porcelain figurines.

On this winter's afternoon a child was standing there, her forehead against the glass, earnest and enormous eyes studying each discarded treasure as if she were looking for something quite special. Finally she straightened up with a satisfied air and entered the store.

The shadowy interior of Pete Richards's establishment was even more cluttered than his show window. Shelves were stacked with jewel caskets, dueling pistols, clocks, and lamps, and the floor was heaped with andirons and mandolins and things hard to find a name for.

Behind the counter stood Pete himself, a man not more than thirty but with hair already turning gray. There was a bleak air about him as he looked at the small customer who flattened her ungloved hands on the counter.

"Mister," she began, "would you please let me look at the string of blue beads in the window?"

Pete parted the draperies and lifted out a necklace. The turquoise stones gleamed brightly against the pallor of his palm as he spread the ornament before her.

"They're just perfect," said the child, entirely to herself. "Will you wrap them up pretty for me, please?"

Pete studied her with a stony air. "Are you buying these for someone?"

"They're for my big sister. She takes care of me. You see, this will be the first Christmas since Mother died. I've been looking for the most wonderful Christmas present for my sister."

"How much money do you have?" asked Pete warily.

She had been busily untying the knots in a handkerchief and now she poured out a handful of pennies on the counter.

"I emptied my bank," she explained simply.

Pete Richards looked at her thoughtfully. Then he carefully drew back the necklace. The price tag was visible to him but not to her. How could he tell her? The trusting look of her blue eyes smote him like the pain of an old wound.

"Just a minute," he said, and turned toward the back of the store. Over his shoulder he called, "What's your name?" He was very busy about something.

"Jean Grace."

When Pete returned to where Jean Grace waited, a package lay in his hand, wrapped in scarlet paper and tied with a bow of green. "There you are," he said shortly. "Don't lose it on the way home."

She smiled happily at him over her shoulder as she ran out the door. Through the window he watched her go, while desolation flooded his thoughts. Something about Jean Grace and her string of beads had stirred him to the depths of a grief that would not stay buried. The child's hair was wheat yellow, her eyes sea blue, and once upon a time, not long before,

Pete had been in love with a girl with hair of that same yellow and with eyes just as blue. And the turquoise necklace was to have been hers.

But there had come a rainy night—a truck skidding on a slippery road—and the life was crushed out of his dream.

Since then Pete Richards had lived too much with his grief in solitude. He was politely attentive to customers, but after hours his world seemed irrevocably empty. He was trying to forget in a self-pitying haze that deepened day by day.

The blue eyes of Jean Grace jolted him into acute remembrance of what he had lost. The pain of it made him recoil from the exuberance of holiday shoppers. During the next ten days trade was brisk; chattering women swarmed in, fingering trinkets, trying to bargain. When the last customer had gone, late on Christmas Eve, he sighed with relief. It was over for another year. But for Pete Richards the night was not quite over.

The door opened and a young woman hurried in. With an inexplicable start, he realized that she looked familiar, yet he could not remember when or where he had seen her before. Her hair was golden yellow and her large eyes were blue. Without speaking, she drew from her purse a package loosely unwrapped in its red paper, a bow of green ribbon with it. Presently the string of blue beads lay gleaming again before him.

"Did this come from your shop?" she asked.

Pete raised his eyes to hers and answered softly, "Yes, it did."

"Are the stones real?"

"Yes. Not the finest quality—but real."

"Can you remember who it was you sold them to?"

"She was a small girl. Her name was Jean. She bought them for her older sister's Christmas present."

"How much are they worth?"

"The price," he told her solemnly, "is always a confidential matter between the seller and the customer."

"But Jean has never had more than a few pennies of spending money. How could she pay for them?"

Pete was folding the gay paper back into its creases, rewrapping the little package just as neatly as before.

"She paid the biggest price anyone can ever pay," he said. "She gave all she had."

There was a silence then that filled the little curio shop. He saw the faraway steeple, a bell began ringing. The sound of the distant chiming, the little package lying on the counter, the question in the eyes of the girl, and the strange feeling of renewal struggling unreasonably in the heart of the man, all had come to be because of the love of a child.

"But why did you do it?"

He held out the gift in his hand.

"It's already Christmas morning," he said. "And it's my misfortune that I have no one to give anything to. Will you let me see you home and wish you a Merry Christmas at your door?"

And so, to the sound of many bells and in the midst of happy people, Pete Richards and a girl whose name he had yet to hear, walked out into the beginning of the great day that brings hope into the world for us all.

AN EXCHANGE OF GIFTS

Diane Rayner

I grew up believing that Christmas was a time when strange and wonderful things happened, when wise and royal visitors came riding, when at midnight the barnyard animals talked to one another, and in the light of a fabulous star God came down to us as a child. Christmas to me has always been a time of enchantment, and never more so than the year my son Marty was eight.

That was the year my children and I moved into a cozy trailer home in a forested area just outside of Redmond, Washington. As the holiday approached, our lightened spirits could not be dampened even by the winter rains that swept down Puget Sound to douse our home and make our floors muddy.

Throughout that December, Marty had been the most spirited and busiest of us all. He was my youngest, a cheerful boy, blond and playful, with a quaint habit of looking up at you and cocking his head like a puppy when you spoke to him. The reason for this was that Marty was deaf in his left ear, but it was a condition he never complained about.

For weeks I had been watching Marty. I knew something was going on that he was not telling me about. I saw how eagerly he made his bed, took out the trash, and carefully set the table and helped Rick and Pam prepare dinner before I got home from work. I saw how he silently collected his allowance and tucked it away, not spending a cent of it. I had no idea what all this quiet activity was about, but I suspected it had something to do with Kenny.

Kenny was Marty's friend, and ever since they had found each other in the springtime, they were seldom apart. If you called to one, you got them both. Their world was in the meadow—a horse pasture broken by a small winding stream—where they caught frogs and snakes, searched for arrowheads and hidden treasures, or spent afternoons feeding peanuts to squirrels.

Times were hard for our family, and we had to do some scrimping to get by. Thanks to my job as a meat wrapper and a lot of ingenuity, we managed to have elegance on a shoestring. But not Kenny's family. They were desperately poor, and his mother was struggling to feed and clothe her two children. They were a good, solid family; but Kenny's mom was a proud woman, and she had strict rules.

How we worked, as we did each year, to make our home festive for the holiday! Ours was a hand-crafted Christmas of gifts hidden away and ornaments strung about the place.

Marty and Kenny sometimes sat still at the table long enough to help make cornucopias or weave baskets for the tree; but then one whispered to the other, and they were out the door in a flash, sliding cautiously under the electric fence into the horse pasture that separated our home from Kenny's.

One night shortly before Christmas, when my hands were deep in *peppernoder* dough, shaping the nutlike Danish cookies heavily spiced with cinnamon, Marty came to me and said in a tone mixed with pleasure and pride, "Mom, I've bought Kenny a Christmas present. Want to see it?"

So that's what he's been up to, I thought.

"It's something he's wanted for a long, long time, Mom."

After carefully wiping his hands on a dish towel, he pulled a small box from his pocket. Lifting the lid, I gazed at the pocket compass my son had been saving all those allowances to buy.

"It's a lovely gift, Martin," I said, but even as I spoke, a disturbing thought came to mind. I knew how Kenny's mother felt about their poverty. They could barely afford to exchange gifts among themselves, and giving presents to others was out of the question. I was sure she would not permit her son to receive something he could not return in kind.

Gently, carefully, I talked over the problem with Marty. He understood what I was saying.

"I know, Mom, I know. . .but what if it was a *secret?* What if they never found out *who* gave it?"

I didn't know how to answer him.

The day before Christmas was rainy, cold, and gray. The three kids and I all but fell over one another as we elbowed our way about our home putting finishing touches on secret Christmas gifts and preparing for family and friends who would drop by.

Night settled in. The rain continued. I looked out the window over the sink and felt an odd sadness. How mundane the rain seemed for Christmas Eve. Would wise men come on such a night? I doubted it. It seemed to me that strange and wonderful things happened only on clear nights, nights when one could at least see a star in the heavens.

I turned from the window, and as I checked on the ham and *lefse* bread warming in the oven, I saw Marty slip out the door. He wore his coat over his pajamas, and he clutched a tiny, colorfully wrapped box.

Down through the soggy pasture he went, then under the electric fence and across the yard to Kenny's house. Up the steps on tiptoe, shoes squishing; open the screen door just a crack; place the gift on the doorstep; then take a deep breath, reach for the doorbell and press it *hard.*

Quickly Marty turned and ran down the steps and across the yard in a wild race to get away unnoticed. Then, suddenly, he banged into the electric fence.

The shock sent him reeling. He lay stunned on the wet ground. His body tingled and he gasped for breath. Then slowly, weakly, confused and frightened, he began the grueling trip back home.

"Marty," I cried as he stumbled through the door, "what happened?" His lower lip quivered, his eyes brimmed.

"I forgot about the fence, and it knocked me down!"

I hugged his muddy body to me. He was still dazed, and there was a red mark beginning to blister on his face from his mouth to his ear. Quickly I treated the blister and, with a warm cup of cocoa soothing him, Marty's bright spirits returned. I tucked him into bed and just before he fell asleep he looked up at me and said, "Mom, Kenny didn't see me. I'm sure he didn't see me."

That Christmas Eve I went to bed unhappy and puzzled. It seemed such a cruel thing to happen to a little boy who was doing what the Lord wants us all to do, giving to others, and giving in secret at that. I did not sleep well that night. Somewhere deep inside I must have been feeling the disappointment that Christmas had come and it had been just an ordinary, problem-filled night, no mysterious enchantment at all.

But I was wrong. By morning the rain stopped and the sun shone. The streak on Marty's face was red, but I could tell that the burn was not serious. We opened our presents, and soon, not unexpectedly, Kenny was knocking on the door, eager to show Marty his new compass and tell about the mystery of its arrival. It was plain that Kenny didn't suspect Marty at all, and while the two of them talked, Marty just smiled and smiled.

Then I noticed that while the two boys were comparing their

Christmases, nodding and gesturing and chattering away, Marty was not cocking his head when Kenny was talking. Marty seemed to be listening with his deaf ear. Weeks later a report came from the school nurse, verifying what Marty and I already knew: "Marty now has complete hearing in both ears."

How Marty regained his hearing, and still has it, remains a mystery. Doctors suspect that the shock from the electric fence was somehow responsible. Perhaps so. Whatever the reason, I am thankful to God for the good exchange of gifts that was made that night.

So you see, strange and wonderful things still happen on the night of our Lord's birth. And one does not have to have a clear night in order to follow a fabulous star.

THE SPIRIT OF CHRISTMAS
Retold by Marilyn McAuley

D r. Norman Vincent Peale once told a story about a twelve-year-old boy and his father who were doing some last-minute Christmas shopping. They were caught up in the bustling crowd and moving quickly when, suddenly, the boy flinched. An old beggar had touched his arm, hoping the boy would give him some money.

The wise father saw what happened and took the boy aside to explain that he should have a more compassionate attitude. His son didn't agree. He saw the old man as nothing more than a dirty bum, but the father saw him as a human being. Pressing a large bill into his son's hand, the boy was encouraged to give it to the beggar in the spirit of Christmas.

The boy obeyed his father and when the old beggar received the generous sum, he seemed to stand taller. Suddenly his face took on character and his eyes twinkled. The boy was startled at the dramatic change. The old man bowed to the boy and thanked him—and in the spirit of Christmas he added, "May God bless you."

The boy learned a lesson that would stay with him the rest of his life. That day he realized that dignity rests in the soul of every human being, regardless of the outward appearance.

Dr. Peale would know—for he was that boy.

NATIVITY
Philip Gulley

My mother-in-law, Ruby, lives in southern Indiana in the town of Paoli. We spend family Christmas with her. Those good people in Paoli remember what Christmas is all about. Each year, just before Thanksgiving, Herb from the street department hauls the baby Jesus, his mommy and daddy, and an assortment of livestock and wise men out of storage and sets them up on the courthouse lawn. The Holy Family takes up residence on the southwest corner of the square and no one dares complain.

But Christmas isn't official until Wilson Roberts decorates his variety store, which he does on the day after Thanksgiving. Each year it was the same adornments—a cardboard cutout of Rudolph taped to the front window, a strand of tinsel hung over the checkout counter, and a bucket of candy canes left over from the year before sitting next to the cash register. On that day, at precisely 8:50 A.M., people all over town head to the variety store to start their gift-buying. It is a migration every bit as predictable as the Capistrano swallows.

I stopped in a few years ago looking for a nativity set. The week before, my wife had said, "What this house needs is a nativity set." So on the day after Thanksgiving, while everyone else was lying around in a turkey-filled stupor, I drove into town to the variety store. It's a small store, in sore need of a liquidation sale. Wilson's motto is "We have it, if we can find it." Forty years of merchandise is stacked to the ceiling. It makes for some incongruent discoveries. I once found a poster of Michael Jackson next to a 1959 edition of the *Farmer's Almanac*.

I went inside and sought out Mr. Roberts. He was sitting in the back of the store, smoking a cigar, his ashes dribbling on the wood floor.

"I'd like to buy a nativity set," I told him.

He said, "Well, I know we have one, if we can just find it."

He began to look. He looked over by the hair nets and bobby pins. Not there. He looked by the garden hoses. Not there. Then over by the yard goods and notions. No Holy Family there, either. He looked over near the lawn chairs, then underneath the candy display, which is where he found it.

He dusted off the box, opened it, and took a roll call. One manger, one kneeling mother, one proud father, three wise men, one sheep, one cow, one donkey, and one baby Jesus. Everyone present and accounted for.

"That'll be twelve dollars," he told me.

"How about ten?" I countered. The box was torn and the cow was missing an ear.

Wilson Roberts squinted at me, shifted his cigar from one side of his mouth to the other, then said, "You got a deal." So now we have a nativity set. French made, genuine plaster from Paris, the box says.

The day I bought the nativity set was the last time I saw Wilson Roberts alive. He died the next year. We drive past his old store on our way to Thanksgiving dinner at Ruby's. The variety store is closed now. When he died, it died. Then Wal-Mart moved in and people talk like it's a blessing. I guarantee you Wal-Mart won't have a 1959 edition of the *Farmer's Almanac*. Don't even bother to ask.

I think back on Wilson Roberts searching amidst bobby pins and yard goods for the baby Jesus. Sometimes our search for the Divine has us poking around in all kinds of corners.

Every year at Christmas, I haul our nativity set out of storage and set it on the piano next to our front door. That way when we're scurrying about in a frenzy honoring the birth of the One who told us not to be anxious about anything, we can pause and remember what Christmas is all about.

CHRISTMAS WITHOUT GRANDMA KAY

Robin Jones Gunn

Okay," I agreed with my husband, Ross. "We'll invite your family here for Christmas. But you know it's going to be hard for everyone since your mom passed away."

"I know," he said. "That's why we all need to be together." I sort of agreed with him. But I knew I couldn't take Kay's place as hostess. I was still grieving myself and didn't feel I could be responsible for the emotional atmosphere on our first holiday without her.

I made all the preparations—cookies, decorations, presents—then welcomed Ross's family on Christmas Eve with open arms as I braced myself for a holiday punctuated by sorrow. That evening at church, our clan filled the entire back section. Afterwards, at home, the kids scampered upstairs and Ross shouted, "Five minutes!" The adults settled in the living room and Ross began to read from Luke 2.

At verse eight, our six-year-old, Rachel, appeared at the top of the stairs wearing her brother's bathrobe, a shawl over her head, and carrying a stuffed lamb under her arm. She struck a pose and stared at the light fixture over the dining room table as if an angel had just appeared.

My father-in-law chuckled, "Look at her! You'd think she could really hear heavenly voices."

Next came Mary, one of my nieces who'd donned the blue bridesmaid dress I wore in my sister's wedding. I knew then that the kids had gotten into my closet. The plastic baby Jesus fit nicely under the full skirt of the blue dress. My son, appearing as Joseph, discreetly turned his head as Mary "brought forth" her firstborn son on the living room floor, wrapped him in a dish towel and laid him in the laundry basket.

We heard a commotion as Ross turned to Matthew 2 and read the cue for the Magi. He repeated it, louder: "We saw his star in the east and have come to worship him."

One of my junior-high-age nephews whispered, "You go first!" and pushed his older brother out of the bedroom into full view. Slowly the ultimate wise man descended with Rachel's black tutu on his head and bearing a large bottle of canola oil.

The adults burst out laughing and I did, too, until I realized what he was wearing. It was a gold brocade dress with pearls and sequins that circled the neck and shimmered down the entire left side. Obviously the kids had gone through the bags I'd brought home after we cleaned out Kay's closet. Bags filled with shoes, hats, a few dresses and some scarves that still smelled like her.

The laughter quickly diminished when my father-in-law said, "Hey! That's Kay's dress! What are you doing wearing her dress?"

Rachel looked at Grandpa from her perch at the top of the staircase. "Grandma doesn't mind if he uses it," she said. "I know she doesn't."

We all glanced silently at each other.

I didn't doubt that Rachel had an inside track into her grandma's heart. Kay had been there the day she was born, waiting all night in the hospital, holding a vase with two pink roses picked from her garden. She'd carried the roses through two airports and on the hour-long flight, telling everyone who she was going to see: "My son, his wife, my grandson and the granddaughter I've been waiting for."

I'd slept with the two pink roses on my nightstand and my baby girl next to me in her bassinet. When I awoke early in the morning to nurse my squirming, squealing infant, I noticed a red mark on her cheek. Was it blood? A birthmark I hadn't noticed before?

No, it was lipstick. Grandma Kay had visited her first granddaughter sometime during the night.

It was Grandma Kay who taught Rachel the three silent squeezes. A squeeze-squeeze-squeeze of the hand means, "I love you." My first introduction to the squeezes was in the bride's dressing room on my wedding day. Kay slid past the wedding coordinator and photographer. In all the flurry, she quietly slipped her soft hand into mine and squeezed it three times. After that, I felt the silent squeezes many times. We all did.

When we got the call last year that Kay had gone into a diabetic coma, Ross caught the next plane home. Our children and I prayed this would only be a close call, like so many others the past two years. But Kay didn't come out of it this time. A week later, we tried to accept the doctor's diagnosis that it was only a matter of days. The children seemed to understand that all we could do was wait.

One night that week, Rachel couldn't sleep. I brought her to bed with me but she wouldn't settle down. Crying, she said she wanted to talk to her Grandma.

"Just have Daddy put the phone up to her ear," she pleaded. "I know she'll hear me."

It was 10:30 P.M. I called the hospital and asked for Kay's room. My husband answered at her bedside. I watched my daughter sit up straight and take a deep breath.

"Okay, Rachel," my husband said. "You'll have to talk loud because there are noisy machines helping Grandma breathe."

"Grandma, it's me, Rachel!" she shouted. "I wanted to tell you good night. I'll see you in heaven."

Rachel handed me the phone and nestled down under the covers.

"Oh," she said, springing up. "Tell Daddy to give Grandma three squeezes for me."

Two days later, Grandma Kay died....

Now, Christmas Eve, in our snow-covered house, Rachel was the first to welcome Grandma's memory into our celebration.

"Really, Grandpa," she continued to plead. "Grandma wouldn't mind."

We all knew Rachel was right. Grandma Kay wouldn't have cared if her grandchildren found delight in anything that belonged to her. If the dress had been embroidered with pure 14-karat gold, Grandma Kay wouldn't have minded a bit.

Grandpa nodded. The pageant continued. The next wise guy paraded down the stairs, stumbling on his too-big bathrobe and bearing a jumbo-sized Lawry's Seasoned Salt. He laid it at the laundry basket.

My husband read about the shepherds returning, "glorifying and praising God for all the things they had heard and seen, just as they had been told."

Then the cast took a bow and scrambled for the kitchen where they fought over lighting the candle on Jesus' birthday cake.

When we started singing Happy Birthday to Jesus, I looked down at the little shepherdess standing next to me.

Rachel's small, warm hand nuzzled its way into mine. I knew Grandma Kay was there, too, when I felt three silent squeezes.

MY CHRISTMAS MIRACLE
Taylor Caldwell

For many of us, one Christmas stands out from all the others, the one when the meaning of the day shone clearest.

Although I did not guess it, my own "truest" Christmas began on a rainy spring day in the bleakest year of my life. Recently divorced, I was in my 20s, had no job, and was on my way downtown to go the rounds of the employment offices. I had no umbrella, for my old one had fallen apart, and I could not afford another one. I sat down in the streetcar—and there against the seat was a beautiful silk umbrella with a silver handle inlaid with gold and flecks of bright enamel. I had never seen anything so lovely.

I examined the handle and saw a name engraved among the golden scrolls. The usual procedure would have been to turn in the umbrella to the conductor, but on impulse I decided to take it with me and find the owner myself. I got off the streetcar in a downpour and thankfully opened the umbrella to protect myself. Then I searched a telephone book for the name on the umbrella and found it. I called and a lady answered.

Yes, she said in surprise, that was her umbrella, which her parents, now dead, had given her for a birthday present. But, she added, it had been stolen from her locker at school (she was a teacher) more than a year before. She was so excited that I forgot I was looking for a job and went directly to her small house. She took the umbrella, and her eyes filled with tears.

The teacher wanted to give me a reward, but—though twenty dollars was all I had in the world—her happiness at retrieving this special possession was such that to have accepted money would have spoiled something. We talked for a while, and I must have given her my address. I don't remember.

The next six months were wretched. I was able to obtain only temporary employment here and there, for a small salary, though this was what they now call the Roaring Twenties. But I put aside twenty-five or fifty cents when I could afford it for my little girl's Christmas presents. (It took me six months to save eight dollars.) My last job ended the day before Christmas, my thirty-dollar rent was soon due, and I had fifteen dollars to my name—which Peggy and I would need for food. She was home from her convent boarding school and was excitedly looking forward to her gifts the next day, which I had already purchased. I had bought her a small tree, and we were going to decorate it that night.

The stormy air was full of the sound of Christmas merriment as I walked from the streetcar to my small apartment. Bells rang and children shouted in the bitter dusk of the evening, and windows were lighted and everyone was running and laughing. But there would be no Christmas for me, I knew, no gifts, no remembrance whatsoever. As I struggled through the snowdrifts, I had just about reached the lowest point in my life. Unless a miracle happened, I would be homeless in January, foodless, jobless. I had prayed steadily for weeks, and there had been no answer but this coldness and darkness, this harsh air, this abandonment. God and men had completely forgotten me. I felt old as death, and as lonely. What was to become of us?

I looked in my mailbox. There were only bills in it, a sheaf of them, and two white envelopes which I was sure contained more bills. I went up three dusty flights of stairs, and I cried, shivering in my thin coat. But I made myself smile so I could greet my little daughter with a pretense of happiness. She opened the door for me and threw herself in my arms, screaming joyously and demanding that we decorate the tree immediately.

Peggy had proudly set our kitchen table for our evening meal and put pans out and three cans of food which would be our dinner. For some reason, when I looked at those pans and cans, I felt brokenhearted. We would have only hamburgers for our Christmas dinner tomorrow, and gelatin. I stood in the cold little kitchen, and misery overwhelmed me. For the first time in my life, I doubted the existence of God and his mercy, and the coldness in my heart was colder than ice.

The doorbell rang and Peggy ran fleetly to answer it, calling that it must be Santa Claus. Then I heard a man talking heartily to her and went to the door. He was a delivery man, and his arms were full of parcels, and he was laughing at my child's frenzied joy and her dancing. "This is a mistake," I said, but he read the name on the parcels and they were for me. When he had gone I could only stare at the boxes. Peggy and I sat on the floor and opened them. A huge doll, three times the size of the one I had bought for her. Gloves. Candy. A beautiful leather purse. Incredible! I looked for the name of the sender. It was the teacher, the address simply "California," where she had moved.

Our dinner that night was the most delicious I had ever eaten. I could only pray, "Thank you, Father." I forgot I had no money for the rent and only fifteen dollars in my purse and no job. My child and I ate and laughed together in happiness. Then we decorated the little tree and marveled at it. I put Peggy to bed and set up her gifts around the tree and a sweet peace flooded me like a benediction. I had some hope again. I could even examine the sheaf of bills without cringing. Then I opened the two white envelopes. One contained a check for thirty dollars from a company I had worked for briefly in the summer. It was, said a note, my "Christmas bonus." My rent!

The other envelope was an offer of a permanent position with the government—to begin two days after Christmas. I sat with the letter in my hand and the check on the table before me, and I think that was the most joyful moment of my life up to that time.

The church bells began to ring. I hurriedly looked at my child, who was sleeping blissfully, and ran down to the street. Everywhere people were walking to church to celebrate the birth of the Savior. People smiled at me and I smiled back. The storm had stopped, the sky was pure and glittering with stars.

"The Lord is born!" sang the bells to the crystal night and the laughing darkness. Someone began to sing, "Come, all ye faithful!" I joined in and sang with the strangers all about me.

I am not alone at all, I thought. I was never alone at all.

And that, of course, is the message of Christmas. We are never alone. Not when the night is darkest, the wind coldest, the world seemingly most indifferent. For this is still the time God chooses.

"WHERE'S THE BABY JESUS?"
Jeannie S. Williams

Last December found me filled with the holiday spirit and doing some extensive, elaborate decorating. Our home was part of a Christmas open house tour sponsored by the women of our church to raise money for a local charity.

During the tour one person noticed the small nativity scene on my desk and admired its simplicity and loveliness. After examining it more closely, she noticed the empty manger and asked, "Where's the baby Jesus?"

Her question brought back memories of the year I purchased the broken nativity setting.

I was very bitter and disheartened that year because my parents, after thirty-six years of marriage, were getting a divorce. I could not accept their decision to part and I became depressed, not realizing they needed my love and understanding then more than ever.

My thoughts were constantly filled with childhood memories—the huge Christmas trees, the gleaming decorations, the special gifts, and the love we shared as a close family. Every time I thought about those moments, I'd burst into tears, being sure I'd never feel the spirit of Christmas again.

My children were afraid there wouldn't be any snow for the holidays that year, but two days before Christmas it began to fall. Beautifully and quietly it came during the morning, and by evening it covered everything in sight. I needed to go into town to buy some ribbon and wrapping paper, but I dreaded the idea. Even the new-fallen snow stirred memories of the past.

The store was crowded with last-minute shoppers—pushing, shoving, and complaining as they grabbed from shelves and racks not bothering to put unwanted articles in place. Christmas tree lights and ornaments dangled from open boxes, and the few dolls and stuffed toys reminded me of neglected orphans who had no home. A small nativity scene had fallen to the floor in front of my shopping cart, and I stopped to put it back on the shelf.

After glancing at the endless check-out line, I decided it wasn't worth the effort and had made up my mind to leave when suddenly I heard a loud, sharp voice cry out.

"Sarah! You get that thing out of your mouth right now!"

"But Mommy! I wasn't puttin' it in my mouth! See, Mommy? I was kissin' it! Look, Mommy, it's a little baby Jesus!"

"Well, I don't care what it is! You put it down right now! You hear me?"

"But come look, Mommy," the child insisted. "It's all broken. It's a little manger and the baby Jesus got broked off!"

As I listened from the next aisle, I found myself smiling and wanting to see the little girl who had kissed the baby Jesus. I quietly moved some cartons aside and peeked through a space between the shelves.

She appeared to be about four or five years old and was not properly dressed for the cold, wet weather. Instead of a coat she wore a bulky sweater several sizes too large for her small, slender body. Bright colorful pieces of yarn were tied on the ends of her braids, making her look cheerful despite her ragged attire.

I continued to watch as she clutched the little doll to her cheek, and then she began to hum. Tears slowly filled my eyes as I recognized the melody. Another memory from childhood, a familiar little song: "Away in a manger, no crib for a bed, The little Lord Jesus lay down His sweet head." She had stopped humming and was softly singing the words.

Reluctantly I turned my eyes to her mother. She was paying no attention to the child but was anxiously looking through the marked-down winter coats displayed on the bargain rack near the end of the counter. Like her daughter she was rather shabbily dressed, and her torn, dirty tennis shoes were wet from the cold, melting snow. In her shopping cart was a small baby bundled snugly in a thick, washed-out, yellow blanket, sleeping peacefully.

"Mommy!" the little girl called to her. "Can we buy this here little baby Jesus? We can set Him on the table by the couch and we could..."

"I told you to put that thing down!" her mother interrupted. "You get yourself over here right now, or I'm gonna give you a spankin'. You hear me, girl?"

"But, Mommy!" exclaimed the child. "I bet we could buy it real cheap 'cause it's all broken. You said we ain't gonna get no Christmas tree, so can't we buy this here little baby Jesus instead? Please, Mommy, please?"

Angrily the woman hurried toward the child, and I turned away, not wanting to see, expecting her to punish the child as she had threatened. A few seconds passed as I waited tensely, but I did not hear a sound coming from the next aisle.

No movement, no scolding. Just complete silence. Puzzled, I peered from the corners of my eyes and was astonished to see the mother kneeling on the wet, dirty floor, holding the child close to her trembling body. She struggled to say something but only managed a desperate sob, and the little girl seemed to understand her despair.

"Don't cry, Mommy!" she pleaded. Wrapping her arms around her mother, she nestled her head against the woman's faded jacket and avidly apologized for her behavior. "I'm sorry I wasn't good in this store. I promise I won't ask for nothin' else! I don't want this here little baby Jesus. Really

I don't! See, I'll put Him back here in the manger. Please don't cry no more, Mommy!"

"I'm sorry, too, Honey," answered her mother finally. "You know I don't have enough money to buy anything extra right now, and I'm just crying because I wished I did—it being Christmas and all—but I bet Ole Santa is gonna bring you them pretty little play dishes you been wantin' if you promise to be a real good girl, and maybe next year we can get us a real Christmas tree. How about that! Let's go home now 'fore Jackie wakes up and starts cryin', too." She laughed softly as she hugged her daughter and then kissed her quickly on the forehead.

The little girl was still holding the doll in her hands. She turned to put it on the shelf, glowing with anticipation. The possibility that Santa might bring her a set of dishes was all she needed to be happy once more.

"You know what, Mommy!" she announced excitedly. "I don't really need this here little baby Jesus doll anyhow! You know why? 'Cause my Sunday school teacher says baby Jesus really lives in your heart!"

I looked at the nativity scene and realized that a baby born in a stable some 2,000 years ago was a person who still walks with us today, making His presence known, working to bring us through the difficulties of life, if only we let Him. To share in the glorious wonder of this holiday celebration and to be able to see God in Christ, I knew one must first experience Him in the heart.

"Thank You, God," I began to pray. "Thank You for a wonderful childhood filled with precious memories and for parents who provided a home for me and gave me the love I needed during the most important years of my life, but most of all thank You for giving Your Son."

Quickly I grabbed the nativity scene pieces and hurried to the checkout counter. Recognizing one of the sales clerks, I asked her to give the doll to the little girl who was leaving the store with her mother, explaining I would pay for it later. I watched the child accept the gift and then saw her give "baby Jesus" another kiss as she walked out the door.

Once again the Christmas season will be approaching. Christmas—a time for rejoicing, a time for giving, a time for remembering!

The little broken nativity scene I purchased that evening graces my desk every Christmas. It's there to remind me of a child whose simple words touched my life.

ONCE UPON A CHRISTMASTIME

THE LEGEND OF THE
CHRISTMAS APPLE
Ruth Sawyer

*O*nce upon a time there lived in Germany a little clockmaker by the name of Hermann Joseph. He lived in one little room with a bench for his work, and a chest for his wood, and his tools, and a cupboard for dishes, and a trundle bed under the bench. Besides these there was a stool, and that was all—excepting the clocks.

There were hundreds of clocks: little and big, carved and plain, some with wooden faces and some with porcelain ones—shelf clocks, cuckoo clocks, clocks with chimes and clocks without; and they all hung on the walls, covering them quite up.

In front of his one little window there was a little shelf, and on this Hermann put all his best clocks to show the passersby. Often they would stop and look, and someone would cry: "See, Hermann Joseph has made a new clock. It is finer than any of the rest!"

Then if it happened that anybody was wanting a clock, he would come in and buy it.

I said Hermann was a little clockmaker. That was because his back was bent and his legs were crooked, which made him very short and funny to look at. But there was no kinder face than his in all the city, and the children loved him. Whenever a toy was broken or a doll lost an arm or a leg or an eye, its careless *Mütterchen* would carry it straight to Hermann's little shop.

"The *kindlein* needs mending," she would say. "Canst thou do it now for me?"

And whatever work Hermann was doing he would always put it aside

to mend the broken toy or doll, and never a pfennig would he take for the mending.

"Go spend it for sweetmeats or, better still, put it by till Christmastime. 'Twill get thee some happiness then, maybe," he would always say.

Now it was the custom in that long-ago for those who lived in the city to bring gifts to the great cathedral on Christmas and lay them before the Holy Mother and Child. People saved all through the year that they might have something wonderful to bring on that day; and there was a saying among them that, when a gift was brought that pleased the Christ Child more than any other, He would reach down from Mary's arms and take it.

This was but a saying, of course. The old Herr Graff, the oldest man in the city, could not remember that it had ever really happened; and many there were who laughed at the very idea. But children often talked about it, and the poets made beautiful verses about it; and often when a rich gift was placed beside the altar the watchers would whisper among themselves: "Perhaps now we shall see a miracle."

Those who had no gifts to bring went to the cathedral just the same on Christmas Eve to see the gifts of the others and hear the carols and watch the burning of the waxen tapers. The little clockmaker was one of these. Often he was stopped and someone would ask, "How happens it that you never bring a gift?" Once the Bishop himself questioned: "Poorer than thou have brought offerings to the Child. Where is thy gift?"

Then it was that Hermann had answered: "Wait; someday you shall see. I, too, shall bring a gift someday."

The truth of it was that the little clockmaker was so busy giving what he had all through the year that there was never anything left at Christmastime. But he had a wonderful idea on which he was working every minute that he could spare time from his clocks. It had taken him years and years; no one knew anything about it but Trude, his neighbor's child, and Trude had grown from a baby into a little housemother and still the gift was not finished.

It was a clock, the most wonderful and beautiful clock ever made; and every part of it had been fashioned with loving care. He had spent years carving the case and the hands, years perfecting the works; and now Hermann saw that with a little more haste and time he could finish it for the coming Christmas.

He mended the children's toys as before, but he gave up making his regular clocks, so there were fewer to sell, and often his cupboard was empty and he went supperless to bed. But that only made him a little thinner and his face a little kinder; and meantime the gift clock became more and more beautiful.

It was fashioned after a rude stable with rafters, stall, and crib. The Holy Mother knelt beside the manger in which a tiny Christ Child lay, while through the open door the others came. Three were kings and three were shepherds and three were soldiers and three were angels; and when the hours struck, the figure knelt in adoration before the sleeping Child while the silver chimes played the "Magnificat."

"Thou seest," said the clockmaker to Trude, "it is not just on Sundays and holidays that we should remember to worship the *Krist Kindlein* and bring Him gifts—but every day, every hour."

The days went by like clouds scudding before a winter wind and the clock was finished at last. So happy was Hermann with his work that he put the gift clock on the shelf before the little window to show the passersby. There were crowds looking at it all day long, and many would whisper: "Do you think this can be the gift Hermann has spoken of—his offering on Christmas Eve to the Church?"

The day before Christmas came. Hermann cleaned up his little shop, wound all his clocks, brushed his clothes, and then went over the gift clock again to be sure everything was perfect.

"It will not look meanly beside the other gifts," he thought happily. In fact he was so happy that he gave away all but one pfennig to the blind beggar who passed his door; and then, remembering that he had eaten nothing since breakfast, he spent that last pfennig for a Christmas apple to eat with a crust of bread he had. These he was putting on the cupboard to eat after he was dressed, when the door opened and Trude was standing there crying softly.

"*Kindlein—Kindlein*, what ails thee?" And he gathered her into his arms.

"'Tis Father. He is hurt, and all the money that was put by for the tree and sweets and toys has gone to Herr Doktor. And now, how can I tell the children? Already they have lighted the candle at the window and are waiting for Kris Kringle to come."

The little clockmaker laughed merrily.

"Come, come, little one, all will be well. Hermann will sell a clock for thee. Some house in the city must need a clock; and in a wink we shall have money enough for the tree and the toys. Go home and sing."

He buttoned on his great coat and, picking out the best of the old clocks, he went out. He went first to the rich merchants, but their houses were full of clocks; then to the journeymen, but they said his clock was old-fashioned. He even stood on the corner of the streets and in the square, crying, "A clock—a good clock for sale," but no one paid any attention to him. At last he gathered up his courage and went to the Herr Graff himself.

"Will your Excellency buy a clock?" he said, trembling at his own boldness. "I would not ask, but it is Christmas and I am needing to buy happiness for some children."

Then Herr Graff smiled.

"Yes, I will buy a clock, but not that one. I will pay a thousand gulden for the clock thou hast had in thy window these four days past."

"But your Excellency, that is impossible!" And poor Hermann trembled harder than ever.

"Poof! Nothing is impossible. That clock or none. Get thee home and I will send for it in half an hour and pay thee the gulden."

The little clockmaker stumbled out.

"Anything but that—anything but that!" he kept mumbling over and over to himself on his way home. But as he passed the neighbor's house he saw the children at the window with their lighted candle, and he heard Trude singing.

And so it happened that the servant who came from the Herr Graff carried the gift clock away with him; but the clockmaker would take but five of the thousand gulden in payment to give to Trude. And as the servant disappeared up the street the chimes commenced to ring from the great cathedral, and the streets suddenly became noisy with the many people going thither bearing their Christmas offerings.

"I have gone empty-handed before," said the little clockmaker sadly. "I can go empty-handed once again."

As he turned to shut his cupboard door behind him his eyes fell on the Christmas apple, and an odd little smile crept into the corners of his mouth and lighted his eyes.

"It is all I have—my dinner for two days. I will carry that to the Christ Child. It is better, after all, than going empty-handed."

How full of peace and beauty was the great cathedral when Hermann entered it! There were a thousand tapers burning, and everywhere the sweet scent of the Christmas greens—and the laden altar before the Holy Mother and Child.

There were richer gifts than had been brought for many years: marvelously wrought vessels from the greatest silversmiths; cloth of gold and cloth of silk brought from the East by the merchants; poets had brought their songs illuminated on rolls of heavy parchment; painters had brought their pictures of saints and the Holy Family; even the King himself had brought his crown and scepter to lay before the Child. And after all these offerings came the little clockmaker, walking slowly down the long, dim aisle, holding tight to his Christmas apple.

The people saw him and a murmur rose, hummed a moment indistinctly through the church, and then grew clear and articulate: "Shame! See, he is too mean to bring his clock! He hoards it as a miser hoards his gold. See what he brings! Shame!"

The words reached Hermann but he stumbled on, his head dropped forward nearly to his breast, his hands groping the way. The distance seemed interminable for his little bent body. Now he knew he was past the seats; now his feet touched the first step, and there were seven to climb to the altar. Would his feet never reach the top?

"One, two, three," he counted to himself. "Four, five, six." He was nearly there. There was but one more.

The murmur of shame died away and in its place rose one of wonder and awe. Soon the words became intelligible: "The miracle! It is the miracle!"

The people knelt in the big cathedral; the Bishop raised his hands in prayer. And the little clockmaker, stumbling on the last step, looked up through dim eyes and saw the Child leaning toward him, far down from Mary's arms, with hands outstretched to take his gift.

THE CHRISTMAS GUEST

Edwin Markham

ADAPTED FROM *HOW THE GREAT GUEST CAME*

It happened one day near December's end,
Two neighbors called on an old-time friend,
And they found his shop so meager and poor,
Made bright with boughs from ceiling to floor,
And Conrad was sitting with face a-shine—
When he suddenly stopped as he stitched a twine
And said, "Old Friends, at dawn today,
When the cock was crowing the night away—
The Lord appeared in a dream to me—
And said, 'I am coming your guest to be!'
So I've been busy with feet astir,
Strewing my shop with branches of fir.
The table is spread and the kettle is shined,
And over the rafters the holly is twined—
And now I will wait for my Lord to appear
And listen closely so I will hear
His step as he nears my humble place—
Then I'll open the door and look on his face."

So his friends went home and left Conrad alone,
For this was the happiest day he had known.
For long since his family had passed away,
And Conrad had spent many a sad Christmas Day.

But he knew with the Lord as his great guest,
This Christmas would be the dearest and best.
So he listened with only joy in his heart,
And with every sound he would rise with a start
And look for the Lord to be at the door
Like the dream he had a few hours before.

So he ran to the window after hearing a sound,
But all he could see on the snow-covered ground
Was a shabby beggar whose shoes were torn—
And all of his clothes were ragged and worn;
But Conrad was touched and went to the door,
And he said, "Your feet must be frozen and sore—
I have some shoes in my shop for you,
And a coat that will keep you warmer, too."

So with grateful heart the man went away—
But Conrad noticed the time of day;
He wondered what made the dear Lord so late
And how much longer he'd have to wait—
Then he heard a knock and ran to the door,
But it was only a stranger once more,
A bent old lady with a shawl of black,
And a bundle of kindling piled on her back.
She asked for only a place to rest—
But that was reserved for Conrad's great guest,
Yet her voice seemed to plead, "Don't send me away,
Let me rest for a while on this Christmas Day."

So Conrad brewed her a steaming cup
And told her to sit at the table and sup.
But after she left, he was filled with dismay,
For he saw that the hours were slipping away,
And the Lord had not come as he said he would
And Conrad felt sure he had misunderstood.
When out of the stillness he heard a cry,
"Please help me and tell me where am I."
So again he opened his friendly door,
And stood disappointed as twice before.
It was only a child who had wandered away
And was lost from her family on Christmas Day.
Again Conrad's heart was heavy and sad
But he knew he could make this little girl glad.
So he called her in and wiped her tears
And quieted all her childish fears,
Then he led her back to her home once more,
But as he entered his own darkened door,
He knew that the Lord was not coming today
For the hours of Christmas had passed away.
So he went to his room and knelt down to pray,
And Condrad asked, "Lord, why did you delay?
What kept you from coming to call on me,
For I wanted so much your face to see."
Then soft in the silence, a voice he heard,
"Lift up your head for I kept my word.
Three times my shadow crossed your floor,
Three times I came to your lowly door;

For I was the beggar with bruised cold feet;
I was the woman you gave something to eat;
And I was the child on the homeless street.
Three times I knocked, three times I came in,
And each time I found the warmth of a friend.
Of all the gifts, love is the best;
I was honored to be your Christmas Guest."

What can I give him

Poor as I am;

If I were a shepherd,

I would give him a lamb.

If I were a wise man,

I would do my part.

But what can I give him?

I will give him my heart.

Christina Rossetti

THE SECRET OF THE GIFTS
Paul Flucke

he story has been told for centuries now. The story of Caspar, Melchior, and Balthasar and the gifts they brought to the newborn king. And of how they saw the star and followed it for weeks, across mountain and valley and desert. In stately procession on their swaying beasts, they came and placed their treasures at the feet of the infant Savior.

And what were their gifts. Ah, you say, everyone knows. They brought gold, frankincense, and myrrh. So it has been told.

But that is not the whole story. Listen to the rest and you shall learn the secret of the gifts.

The first of the three visitors to approach was Caspar. His cloak was of the finest velvet, trimmed in flawless fur. At his throat were clusters of gems, for Caspar was a wealthy man.

Those who watched saw only that he paused at the door. "He prays," they whispered to one another as they saw Caspar's lips move. But they were mistaken. They could not see that it was the Angel Gabriel, guarding the holy place, before whom Caspar stopped.

"All who enter must bring a gift," said Gabriel. "Have you a gift?"

"Indeed I have," said Caspar, and he held aloft a finely wrought box. It was small, yet so heavy that his arms could hardly raise it. "I have brought bars of the purest gold."

"Your gift," said Gabriel somberly, "must be something of the essence of yourself. It must be something precious to your soul."

"Such have I brought," answered Caspar confidently, the hint of a smile upon his lips.

"So shall it be," said Gabriel. And he, too, smiled as he held the door for Caspar to enter.

Caspar advanced a step, and then another. He was just about to kneel and lay his gold before the child when he stopped and stood erect. There in his outstretched hands lay not gold, but a hammer. Its scarred and blackened head was larger than a man's fist. And its handle was of sinewy wood, as long as a man's forearm.

"But, but—" Caspar stammered as he stared, dumfounded, at the heavy tool. And then softly, from behind him, he heard the voice of Gabriel.

"So shall it be, and so it is," said the angel. "You have brought the essence of yourself. What you hold in your hands is the hammer of your greed. You have used it to pound wealth from those who labor so that you may live in luxury. You have used it to build a mansion for yourself while others dwell in hovels."

And suddenly Caspar knew the truth. Bowed with shame, he turned toward the door to leave. But Gabriel blocked the way. "No, you have not offered your gift."

"Give *this?*" Caspar blurted in horror, looking at the hammer. "I cannot give this to a king!"

"But you must," Gabriel replied. "This is why you came. And you cannot take it back with you. It's too heavy. Leave it here or it will destroy you."

And once again, Caspar knew the angel spoke the truth. But still he protested. "The hammer is too heavy. Why, the child cannot lift it."

"He is the only one who can," replied the angel.

"But it is dangerous. He might bruise his hands or feet."

"That worry," said Gabriel, "you must leave to heaven. The hammer shall find its place." Slowly Caspar turned to where the Christ child lay. And slowly he placed the ugly hammer at the baby's feet. Then he rose and turned to the door, pausing only for an instant to look back at the tiny Savior before he rushed outside.

The waiting world saw only the smile that wreathed Caspar's face as he emerged. His hands were raised, as though the wings of angels graced his fingers.

Next to step to the door was Melchior. He was not so resplendent as Caspar, for he wore the darker robes of the scholar. But the length of his beard and the furrows in his brow bespoke one who had lived long with the wisdom of the ages. A hush fell over the onlookers as he, too, paused before the door. But only Melchior could see the angel who stood guard. Only Melchior could hear him speak.

"What have you brought?" asked Gabriel.

And Melchior replied, "I bring frankincense, the fragrance of hidden lands and bygone days."

"Your gift," cautioned Gabriel as he had done before, "must be something precious to your soul."

"Of course it is," retorted Melchior.

"Then enter, and we shall see." And Gabriel opened the door.

Melchior stood breathless before the scene within. In all his many years of searching for elusive Truth, he had never sensed such a presence as this. He knelt reverently. And from beneath his robe he withdrew the silver flask of precious ointment.

But then he drew back and stared. The vessel in his hand was not silver at all. It was common clay, rough and stained as might be found in the humblest cupboard. Aghast, he pulled the stopper from its mouth and sniffed the contents. Then he leapt to his feet, only to face the angel at the door.

"I have been tricked," he said, spitting the words with fury. "This is not the frankincense I brought! This is vinegar!" Melchior snarled as though it were a curse.

"So shall it be, and so it is," said Gabriel. "You have brought what you are made of. You bring the bitterness of your heart, the soured wine of a life turned grim with jealousy and hate. You have carried within you too long the memory of old hurts. You have hoarded your resentments and breathed on sparks of anger until they have become as embers smoldering within you. You have sought knowledge. But you have filled your life with poison."

As he heard these words, Melchior's shoulders drooped. He turned his face away from Gabriel and fumbled with his robe, as though to hide the earthen jar. Silently he sidled toward the door.

Gabriel smiled gently and placed his hand on Melchior's arm. "Wait," he said. "You must leave your gift."

Melchior sighed with a pain that came from deep within him. "How I wish I could! How long have I yearned to empty my soul of its bitterness. You have spoken the truth, my friend. But I cannot leave it here! Not here, at the feet of love and innocence."

"But you can," said Gabriel. "And you must, if you would be clean. This is the only place you *can* leave it."

"This is vile and bitter stuff," Melchior protested. "What if the child should touch it to his lips?"

"You must leave that worry to heaven," Gabriel replied. "There is use even for vinegar."

So Melchior placed his gift before the Savior. And they say that when he came out, his eyes shown with the clearest light of heaven's truth.

There was yet one more visitor to make his offering. He strode forward now, his back as straight as a tree, shoulders firm as an oaken beam. He walked as one born to command. This was Balthasar, leader of many legions, scourge of walled cities. Before him, as he grasped it by its handle of polished ebony, he carried a brass-bound box.

A murmur ran through those who watched as they saw him hesitate before the door. "Look," they whispered, "even the great Balthasar does obeisance before the king who waits within."

But it was Gabriel who caused the warrior to pause.

"Have you a gift?"

"Of course," answered Balthasar. "I bring a gift of myrrh, the most precious booty of my boldest conquest. Many have fought and died for such as this. It is the essence of the rarest herb."

"But is it the essence of yourself?" asked Gabriel.

"It is," replied the general.

"Then come," said the angel, "and we shall see."

Even the fearless Balthasar was not prepared for the wave of awe that struck him as he entered. He felt a weakness in his knees such as he had never known. Closing his eyes, he knelt and shuffled forward in reverence. Then, bowing until his face was near the ground, he slowly released his grip upon the handle of the box and raised his head and opened his eyes.

What lay before the baby's feet was his own spear. Its smooth round staff still glistened where the sweat of his palms had moistened it. And the razor edges of its steely tip caught the flickering light of the lamp.

"It cannot be!" Balthasar whispered hoarsely. "Some enemy has cast a spell."

"That is more true than you know," said Gabriel softly from behind him. "A thousand enemies have cast their spell on you and turned your soul into a spear. Living only to conquer, you have been conquered. Each battle you win leads you only to another with a foe yet more formidable."

Balthasar heard the angel's words and they seemed to echo in the deepest places of his soul. For a moment, he hesitated. Then, taking control of himself, he reached down and grasped his spear—and turned toward the door.

"I cannot leave this here," he said. "My people need it. We cannot afford to give it up."

"Are you sure," asked Gabriel, "that you can afford to *keep* it?"

A long moment passed. Finally Balthasar loosed his grip, and the spear drooped toward the floor. But as he looked at the child, he whispered anxiously to Gabriel, "But here? Is it safe to leave it here?"

The angel released a long-held breath as he whispered back, "This is the only safe place to leave it."

"But he is a child, and the spear is sharp. It could pierce his flesh."

"That fear you must leave to heaven," Gabriel replied.

And they say that Balthasar left calmly, his arms hanging gently at his sides. They say that he walked first to Caspar and Melchior, where they waited, and embraced them as brothers. Then, turning to the others who watched, he went first to one and then to the next, enfolding each in his outstretched arms as one greeting beloved friends whom he has not seen for a very long time.

But what of their gifts, you ask....What of the hammer and the vinegar and the spear? Another story tells how they were seen once more, years later, on a lonely hill outside Jerusalem. But do not worry. That is a burden heaven took upon itself, as only heaven can.

THE LEGEND OF THE ROBIN
An old French folktale

The winter wind blew harshly, whistling through the walls of the weather-beaten old stable. Mary sat quietly, gazing upward through a hole in the roof at the multitude of stars that twinkled around the greatest, most radiant star she had ever seen. How easily it outshone all the others, as it cast its glorious beam down over the spot where Mary held her newborn babe in her arms.

Mary shivered slightly as she drew her child up close to her, trying to keep him warm. Just in front of them lay a small pile of embers, barely glowing. From time to time, she would bend down and blow on them, ever so slightly, just enough to revive a bit of flame. Somewhere out in the chill darkness Joseph looked for firewood so that they could have a fire to ward off the damp and cold.

Mary tried to blow on the embers while holding the child in her arms, but it was difficult to bend so low and not disturb the child. She looked around the stable, not sure of what to do.

Nearby, sleeping side by side, were a large gray ox, a cart horse, and a donkey. They looked quite cozy, snuggled close together, and the sounds of their snoring filled the stable.

"Please wake up, dear ox," Mary called. "You are so big and strong. Couldn't you blow on these embers with your great breath? I would be so grateful."

Certainly the ox would have helped if he had heard Mary. But he had spent the day working hard in the fields. And he was too tired to hear the gentle voice calling him.

"Faithful horse," Mary said, "you are so proud and tall. Could you use your powerful breath to keep these embers from going out?"

But the horse had spent a long day pulling heavy carts through the streets. Just at this moment she was dreaming of sweet apples and fragrant hay.

"Excuse me, donkey," Mary tried a last time. "But you are so determined at everything you do, could you please see if you could keep these embers burning?"

Now, nobody sleeps more soundly than a donkey. He twitched his ears and gave a huge yawn in his sleep.

Mary sighed and looked at the sleeping animals. She knew how hard they had worked and how tired they must be. So she tried again to bend closer to the fading embers.

Mary did not see the robin who had been watching the whole scene from the rafters above. As Mary tried again to revive her small fire, the little brown bird flew down to the stable floor, alighting right next to the pile of embers.

The little bird drew back her wings, and with all her might began beating them back and forth to fan the embers. Little by little, the embers began to glow a hot red until a flame started up, making the faithful little bird's chest glow red in its reflection.

Mary turned to the robin and said, "Dear bird—thank you so much for your thoughtfulness. From now on, you will always wear a breast of red as a sign of the kindness in your heart." The small bird then sang for joy, causing Mary's baby to laugh with delight.

This is why the robin has a red breast to this very day.

THE LEGEND OF ST. NICHOLAS
AND THE GOLD
Retold by Dave Lindstedt

*O*nce upon a time, in a northern Mediterranean town, there lived a husband and wife who became successful merchants. Their shop in the town square bustled with activity. But even though their business was quite profitable, they were heartbroken because they were unable to have any children. As time passed, they prayed that God would give them a child to brighten their later years. At last a son was born. They named him Nicholas and they lavished him with their love.

As Nicholas grew, he spent his afternoons scurrying around the shop with his parents. In the evening, he liked to sit at his father's desk and watch as his father counted the day's proceeds. Always, before he began, Nicholas's father would drop a gold coin into each of three small cloth bags on a corner of the desk.

"This is for tomorrow, Nicholas," he would say, "so you'll always have soup with your bread."

While Nicholas was still a young man, both his parents died. He was able to live comfortably on his inheritance, so he tucked the three bags of gold away "for tomorrow," and as the years passed he forgot about them.

Having been raised in the Church, Nicholas decided to pursue the priesthood and he eventually became bishop of the Christian church of Myra. One morning, as he was walking toward the vestry, he noticed a ragged man kneeling to pray. Nicholas had often seen the man scavenging in the local marketplace and recognized him as a former nobleman who had fallen on hard times.

"Oh God, please help me," the man cried as he prayed. "If I cannot find work, I cannot buy bread. And if I cannot buy bread, I will have to turn my three daughters out on to the streets to fend for themselves."

Nicholas's heart was moved with compassion and he began to pray that God would show him how he could help this poor man and his family. That evening, as he made his way home through the gathering twilight, Nicholas suddenly remembered the bags of gold. *This is for tomorrow, Nicholas, so you will always have soup with your bread.* Excitedly, he rushed to his house and clambered into the attic where the gold was hidden.

Nicholas knew the nobleman would be too proud to take money from him, so he decided to find another way. He took one bag of gold and under the cover of darkness crept to the nobleman's house. To his delight he found a front window open just enough to slip the bag through. A candle flickered in the background, indicating that someone might be inside, so to avoid detection he quickly slid the bag of gold over the sill and ran away.

Not long after, Nicholas was invited to preside at the wedding of the nobleman's eldest daughter, who suddenly had a large dowry. At the wedding, the nobleman regaled the guests with his tale of the miraculous appearance of the bag of gold.

When Nicholas saw the joy that his gift had brought, he resolved to provide a dowry for the second daughter as well. A few nights later, he took another bag of gold and slipped it through the nobleman's window. Again the nobleman was overjoyed, and his middle daughter soon married into a prominent family. Now, the father no longer had to scrounge in the marketplace, and when Nicholas saw him next, the man was wearing a new pair of trousers and a jacket.

After the second wedding, however, the father began to wonder how these "bags from heaven" had been delivered. He determined to watch his window every night in case a bag of gold might appear for his youngest daughter.

Meanwhile, Nicholas decided it was only right that he should give the third daughter a bag of gold as well, even though the nobleman was obviously no longer destitute. That night, a chilly evening in early December, he once again made his way to the open window and tossed his treasure inside. As he fled, however, he heard the vigilant nobleman call out, "Bishop Nicholas! Is it you?"

Nicholas implored the man not to tell anyone about the gold, but the secret could not be kept. The story of Nicholas's generosity soon spread throughout the town. With his newfound fortune, the nobleman was restored to prominence in the local government. To celebrate his gratitude to the kindly bishop, the nobleman declared an annual feast to be held on December 6, and many of the villagers brought gifts to share with those who were in need.

And that is how St. Nicholas became associated with the giving of gifts.

It is good to be children sometimes,

and never better than at Christmas,

when its mighty founder

was a child himself.

Charles Dickens

FRANKINCENSE AND MYRRH
Heywood Broun

Once there were three kings in the East and they were wise men. They read the heavens and they saw a certain strange star by which they knew that in a distant land the King of the world was to be born. The star beckoned to them and they made preparations for a long journey.

From their palaces they gathered rich gifts, gold and frankincense and myrrh. Great sacks of precious stuffs were loaded upon the backs of the camels which were to bear them on their journey. Everything was in readiness, but one of the wise men seemed perplexed and would not come at once to join his two companions, who were eager and impatient to be on their way in the direction indicated by the star.

They were old, these two kings, and the other wise man was young. When they asked him he could not tell why he waited. He knew that his treasuries had been ransacked for rich gifts for the King of Kings. It seemed that there was nothing more which he could give, and yet he was not content.

He made no answer to the old men who shouted to him that the time had come. The camels were impatient and swayed and snarled. The shadows across the desert grew longer. And still the young king sat and thought deeply.

At length he smiled, and he ordered his servants to open the great treasure sack upon the back of the first of his camels. Then he went into a high chamber to which he had not been since he was a child. He rummaged about and presently came out and approached the caravan. In his hand he carried something which glinted in the sun.

The kings thought that he bore some new gift more rare and precious than any which they had been able to find in all their treasure rooms. They bent down to see, and even the camel drivers peered from the backs of the great beasts to find out what it was which gleamed in the sun. They were curious about this last gift for which all the caravan had waited.

And the young king took a toy from his hand and placed it upon the sand. It was a dog of tin, painted white and speckled with black spots. Great patches of paint had worn away and left the metal clear, and that was why the toy shone in the sun as if it had been silver.

The youngest of the wise men turned a key in the side of the little black-and-white dog and then he stepped aside so that the kings and the camel drivers could see. The dog leaped high in the air and turned a somersault. He turned another and another and then fell over upon his side and lay there with a painted grin upon his face.

A child, the son of a camel driver, laughed and clapped his hands, but the kings were stern. They rebuked the youngest of the wise men and he paid no attention but called to his chief servant to make the first of all the camels kneel. Then he picked up the toy of tin and, opening the treasure sack, placed his last gift with his own hands in the mouth of the sack so that it rested safely upon the soft bags of incense.

"What folly has seized you?" cried the eldest of the wise men. "Is this a gift to bear to the King of Kings in the far country?"

And the young man answered and said: "For the King of Kings there are gifts of great richness, gold and frankincense and myrrh.

"But this," he said, "is for the child in Bethlehem."

THE LEGEND OF THE POINSETTIA
Retold by Alice Gray

On Christmas Eve in a small town on the border of Mexico, the light from a dozen candles glowed through a single window of the old adobe church. For years it had been the custom that families would bring a gift on that holy night in remembrance of the Christ Child. From the oldest to the youngest, each family member reverently approached the nativity scene, bowed in adoration, and placed a gift by the altar.

One night, a young orphan boy stood alone outside the church door. He desperately wanted to go in and join the other families who were laying their gifts at the altar, but he was so poor he had nothing to give.

As he stood near the window, he heard music coming from the church organ. As he listened to the beautiful melody, his tender heart was touched with the wonder of Christmas, and he knelt down, alone, outside the church, and bowed his head in prayer.

When the music stopped, he stood up again, thinking he would start walking back to the orphanage. To his amazement, there in the spot where he had knelt to pray a beautiful plant with scarlet leaves and a tiny yellow flower in its center was blooming. He had never seen anything as beautiful as that flower. *The angels have provided a gift for me to present to the Christ Child!* he thought, gently lifting the plant. The young boy then carried the plant into the church, bowed before the manger, and laid it near the altar with the other gifts.

Every year after that the plant bloomed at Christmastime with brilliant red leaves around tiny yellow flowers. The people of the town called it "The Flower of the Holy Night."

A kind family by the last name of Poinsettia eventually adopted the little boy, and he grew up to be very successful in his business. Years later, he returned to the little village he remembered so fondly to help build a new church and school. In return for his generosity, the people from the town gave him a special gift: They presented him with a beautiful plant whose scarlet leaves encircled tiny golden blossoms—a plant which had been renamed for him.

THE LEGEND OF THE
CHRISTMAS ROSE
Retold by Casandra Lindell

A group of people gathered, talking in hushed voices and shuf-
fling their feet in anticipation. Among them were several shepherds who had just come in from the hills surrounding Bethlehem. A host
of angels had sung to them about the baby just inside; they came to the
small stable to honor Him. Every person there, young and old, carried a
gift to give to this baby.

Standing at the edge of the crowd, listening to the story the shepherds
told, a young girl sensed a wonderful realization begin to grow inside of her.
As she heard their story, she knew that this young child must be the
Promise from God. Beginning to tremble with emotion, she desperately
longed to go inside and worship as well.

But she had no gift to offer. Warm tears of disappointment slowly
rolled down her cold cheeks. Falling to the ground, they were quickly
absorbed, unnoticed, by the dry earth. The crowd pressed inside, surrounding the manger and leaving her alone.

Suddenly an angel appeared, softly humming a beautiful tune. The
angel smiled gently at the young girl and began to scatter white roses in her
path. Just as suddenly, the angel was gone.

The young girl gathered the delicate blossoms and, slipping through
the small door, breathed thanksgiving as she lay her gift at the feet of the
Giver of Gifts.

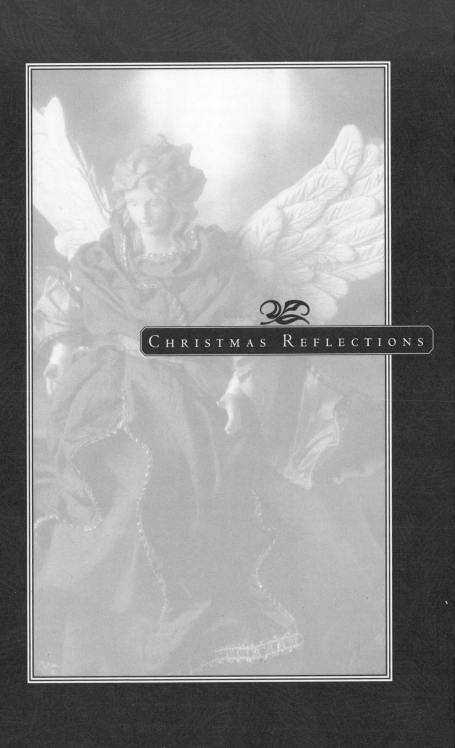

CHRISTMAS REFLECTIONS

THE ARRIVAL

Max Lucado

FROM *GOD CAME NEAR*

The noise and the bustle began earlier than usual in the village. As night gave way to dawn, people were already on the streets. Vendors were positioning themselves on the corners of the most heavily traveled avenues. Store owners were unlocking the doors to their shops. Children were awakened by the excited barking of the street dogs and the complaints of donkeys pulling carts.

The owner of the inn had awakened earlier than most in the town. After all, the inn was full, all the beds taken. Every available mat or blanket had been put to use. Soon all the customers would be stirring and there would be a lot of work to do.

One's imagination is kindled thinking about the conversation of the innkeeper and his family at the breakfast table. Did anyone mention the arrival of the young couple the night before? Did anyone ask about their welfare? Did anyone comment on the pregnancy of the girl on the donkey? Perhaps. Perhaps someone raised the subject. But, at best, it was raised, not discussed. There was nothing that novel about them. They were, possibly, one of several families turned away that night.

Besides, who had time to talk about them when there was so much excitement in the air? Augustus did the economy of Bethlehem a favor when he decreed that a census should be taken. Who could remember when such commerce had hit the village?

No, it is doubtful that anyone mentioned the couple's arrival or wondered about the condition of the girl. They were too busy. The day was upon them. The day's bread had to be made. The morning's chores had to be done. There was too much to do to imagine that the impossible had occurred.

God had entered the world as a baby.

Yet, were someone to chance upon the sheep stable on the outskirts of Bethlehem that morning, what a peculiar scene they would behold.

The stable stinks like all stables do. The stench of urine, dung, and sheep reeks pungently in the air. The ground is hard, the hay scarce. Cobwebs cling to the ceiling and a mouse scurries across the floor.

A more lowly place of birth could not exist.

Off to one side sits a group of shepherds. They sit silently on the floor, perhaps perplexed, perhaps in awe, no doubt in amazement. Their night watch had been interrupted by an explosion of light from heaven and a symphony of angels. God goes to those who have time to hear him—so on this cloudless night he went to simple shepherds.

Near the young mother sits the weary father. If anyone is dozing, he is. He can't remember the last time he sat down. And now that the excitement has subsided a bit, now that Mary and the baby are comfortable, he leans against the wall of the stable and feels his eyes grow heavy. He still hasn't figured it all out. The mystery of the event puzzles him. But he hasn't the energy to wrestle with the questions. What's important is that the baby is fine and that Mary is safe. As sleep comes he remembers the name the angel told him to use—Jesus. "We will call him Jesus."

Wide awake is Mary. My, how young she looks! Her head rests on the soft leather of Joseph's saddle. The pain has been eclipsed by wonder. She looks into the face of the baby. Her son. Her Lord. His Majesty. At this point in history, the human being who best understands who God is and what he is doing is a teenage girl in a smelly stable. She can't take her eyes off him. Somehow Mary knows she is holding God. So this is he. She remembers the words of the angel, "His kingdom will never end."

He looks like anything but a king. His face is prunish and red. His cry, though strong and healthy, is still the helpless and piercing cry of a baby. And he is absolutely dependent upon Mary for his well-being.

Majesty in the midst of the mundane. Holiness in the filth of sheep manure and sweat. Divinity entering the world on the floor of a stable, through the womb of a teenager and in the presence of a carpenter.

She touches the face of the infant-God. How long was your journey!

This baby had overlooked the universe. These rags keeping him warm were the robes of eternity. His golden throne room had been abandoned in favor of a dirty sheep pen. And worshiping angels had been replaced with kind but bewildered shepherds.

Meanwhile, the city hums. The merchants are unaware that God has visited their planet. The innkeeper would never believe that he had just sent God into the cold. And the people would scoff at anyone who told them the Messiah lay in the arms of a teenager on the outskirts of their village. They were all too busy to consider the possibility.

Those who missed His Majesty's arrival that night missed it not because of evil acts or malice; no, they missed it because they simply weren't looking.

Little has changed in the last two thousand years, has it?

DAILY GIFTS

Charles R. Swindoll

FROM *THE FINISHING TOUCH*

*I*t's not too early to give some things away this Christmas. Not just on Christmas Day, but during all the days leading up to December 25. We could call these daily gifts "our Christmas projects." Maybe one per day from now 'til then. Here are a few suggestions.

Mend a quarrel.

Seek out a forgotten friend.

Dismiss suspicion.

Write a long overdue love note.

Hug someone tightly and whisper, "I love you so."

Forgive an enemy.

Be gentle and patient with an angry person.

Express appreciation.

Gladden the heart of a child.

Find the time to keep a promise.

Make or bake something for someone else—anonymously.

Release a grudge.

Listen.

Speak kindly to a stranger.

Enter into another's sorrow.

Smile. Laugh a little. Laugh a little more.

Take a walk with a friend.

Kneel down and pat a dog.

Read a poem or two to your mate or friend.

Lessen your demands on others.

Play some beautiful music during the evening meal.

Apologize if you were wrong.

Turn off the television and talk.

Treat someone to an ice-cream cone (yogurt would be fine).

Do the dishes for the family.

Pray for someone who helped you when you hurt.

Fix breakfast on Saturday morning.

Give a soft answer even though you feel strongly.

Encourage an older person.

Point out one thing you appreciate most about someone you work with or live near.

Offer to baby-sit for a weary mother.

Give your teacher a break: be especially cooperative.

Let's make Christmas one long, extended gift of ourselves to others. Unselfishly. Without announcement. Or obligation. Or reservation. Or hypocrisy.

This is Christianity, isn't it?

THE BIRTHPLACE OF THE KING
William Barclay

When the Lord of Glory came to this earth, he was born in a cave where men sheltered the beasts. The cave in the Church of the Nativity in Bethlehem may be that same cave, or it may not be. That we will never know for certain. But there is something beautiful in the symbolism that the church where the cave is has a door so low that all must stoop to enter. It is supremely fitting that every man should approach the infant Jesus upon his knees.

ONE SMALL CANDLE
Michael Passons
FROM THE AWARD-WINNING SINGING GROUP AVALON

There are many things in a boy's life that help define him as a man. His first bike, his favorite dog, his secret hiding place, or the way he was raised and the values instilled in him. I feel I am a blessed man to have the kind of upbringing that I had, growing up in a place like Yazoo City, Mississippi.

Yes, I remember my first bike. It was purple—not my favorite color at the time—but it rode like the wind! And trailing not far behind that purple gust was my favorite childhood dog, a matronly collie named (what else?) Lassie. Most every day we would travel together through the woods to my secret place (still a secret), and would discuss the world as we saw it. I did most of the talking, but Lassie was a great listener.

I think the greatest wonder of my formative years had to have been Christmas. Yes, that celebrated day of the year in which little boys acquire such things as bikes, puppies, and the like. I can remember my brother and I waking up on Christmas morning, so excited and running so fast into the living room that we didn't give our eyes time to focus and adjust. I would stand there for what seemed like an eternity, straining to focus on those blurry objects left for me under the tree. In fact, "focus" became a pivotal word for that day.

As her two little boys zeroed in on their bounty, my mother was busy in the kitchen, delicately frosting the two layers of a cake baked the night before.

This was no ordinary cake. It was part of a Passons' family tradition. I can honestly say that the focus of Christmas in our home was never on the presents and holiday cheer, wonderful as those memories may have been. The centerpiece of that day was always and unmistakably the celebration of the birth of Jesus Christ. My parents wanted so much for us boys to know Christmas in its truest sense. That's why, to this day, when I think of my childhood Christmases, the same picture comes to my mind. I visualize a young family of four in a humble little kitchen, in Yazoo City, Mississippi. I see them huddled in a circle, singing, their faces aglow from the faint light of one small candle in the middle of that cake...two young parents gathered with their boys, singing Happy Birthday to the King of the universe.

NEXT TIME IT WILL BE DIFFERENT!

John F. MacArthur Jr.

FROM *GOD WITH US*

THE FIRST TIME JESUS CAME

He came veiled in the form of a child.
A star marked His arrival.
Wise men brought Him gifts.
There was no room for Him.
Only a few attended His arrival.
He came as a baby.

THE NEXT TIME JESUS COMES

He will be recognized by all.
Heaven will be lit by His glory
He will bring rewards for His own.
The world won't be able to contain His glory.
Every eye shall see Him.
He will come as Sovereign King and Lord of all.

JESUS, WHO IS HE?

Tim LaHaye

FROM *JESUS, WHO IS HE?*

No person other than Jesus has been addressed by the following titles, because no other person qualifies for them. Some of these titles were given to Him by angels, others by disciples or followers, or even by Hebrew prophets. No one title fully describes Him. To understand who He really was and who He is in His Second Coming, all must be considered together. One thing is certain: No one else comes close to deserving even one of these titles.

THE ALMIGHTY

THE MIGHTY GOD

THE WORD WAS GOD

MY LORD AND MY GOD

OUR SAVIOR JESUS CHRIST

WONDERFUL

COUNSELOR

THE FATHER OF ETERNITY

THE PRINCE OF PEACE

ALPHA AND OMEGA

FIRST AND LAST

GOD BLESSED FOREVER

THE CHRIST

JEHOVAH

THE BEGINNING AND THE ENDING
THE LORD
SAVIOR
THE HOLY ONE
LORD OF ALL
EMMANUEL
THE WAY, THE TRUTH, THE LIFE
KING OF KINGS
LORD OF LORDS

In the history of the world, no one has ever risen from a carpenter's shop to assume such lofty titles. His life can only be explained by the fact that He was indeed "the Son of God" in a unique sense.

THE GLORY OF HUMILITY

Philip Yancey

FROM *THE JESUS I NEVER KNEW*

I remember sitting one Christmas season in a beautiful auditorium in London listening to Handel's *Messiah*, with a full chorus singing about the day when "the glory of the Lord shall be revealed." I had spent the morning in museums viewing remnants of England's glory—the crown jewels, a solid gold ruler's mace, the Lord Mayor's gilded carriage—and it occurred to me that just such images of wealth and power must have filled the minds of Isaiah's contemporaries who first heard that promise. When the Jews read Isaiah's words, no doubt they thought back with sharp nostalgia to the glory days of Solomon, when "the king made silver as common in Jerusalem as stones."

The Messiah who showed up, however, wore a different kind of glory, the glory of humility.... The God who roared, who could order armies and empires about like pawns on a chessboard, this God emerged in Palestine as a baby who could not speak or eat solid food or control his bladder, who depended on a teenage couple for shelter, food, and love.

In London, looking toward the auditorium's royal box where the queen and her family sat, I caught glimpses of the more typical way rulers stride through the world: with bodyguards, and a trumpet fanfare, and a flourish of bright clothes and flashing jewelry. Queen Elizabeth II had recently visited the United States, and reporters delighted in spelling out the logistics involved: Her four thousand pounds of luggage included two outfits for every occasion, a mourning outfit in case someone died, forty pints of plasma, and white kid leather toilet seat covers. She brought along her own hairdresser, two valets, and a host of other attendants. A brief visit of royalty to a foreign country can easily cost twenty million dollars.

In meek contrast, God's visit to earth took place in an animal shelter with no attendants present and nowhere to lay the newborn king but a feed trough. Indeed, the event that divided history, and even our calendars, into two parts may have had more animal than human witnesses. A mule could have stepped on him. "How silently, how silently, the wondrous gift is given."

For just an instant the sky grew luminous with angels, yet who saw that spectacle? Illiterate hirelings who watched the flocks of others, "nobodies" who failed to leave their names...

In W. H. Auden's poem, *For the Time Being*, the wise men proclaim, "O here and now our endless journey stops." The shepherds say, "O here and now our endless journey starts." The search for worldly wisdom has ended; true life has just begun.

THE ANGELS CALLED IT GOOD NEWS

Larry Libby

FROM *SOMEONE AWESOME*

There came a time—at the best time, the right time—when the mighty Son of God turned His back on all the beauty and happiness of His forever home. And somehow—no one knows just how—He stepped out of Heaven and entered Earth as a baby.

It must have seemed a long way between Heaven and Earth.

It must have been sad to leave such a glorious home.

It must have made the angels wide-eyed and solemn to see the King they love and serve say good-bye and take that long step over the edge of Heaven

—down

    —down

        —down

through black space to the little blue-and-brown planet where you and I live. Did the angels know that the man Jesus would have to die? Did they know that when He grew up His strong, gentle hands would be nailed to a cross of wood? Did they know their King would give up His life for all the wrong, hateful things you and I have done?

Did they know those things? I think they probably did.

But it wasn't long before *they* got to come to Earth, too. Late on a sleepy, star-sprinkled night, those angels peeled back the sky just like you would tear open a sparkling Christmas present. Then, with light and joy pouring out of Heaven like water through a broken dam, they began to shout and sing the message that baby Jesus had been born.

The world had a Savior! The angels called it "Good News," and it was.

It still is…and I'll bet it always will be.

❧

That night some shepherds were in the fields outside the village, guarding their flocks of sheep. Suddenly, an angel of the Lord appeared among them, and the radiance of the Lord's glory surrounded them. They were terribly frightened, but the angel reassured them. "Don't be afraid!" he said. "I bring you good news of great joy for everyone! The Savior—yes, the Messiah, the Lord—has been born tonight in Bethlehem, the city of David! And this is how you will recognize him: You will find a baby lying in a manger, wrapped snugly in strips of cloth!"

Suddenly, the angel was joined by a vast host of others—the armies of heaven—praising God: "Glory to God in the highest heaven, and peace on earth, to all who God favors."

LUKE 2:8–14

NEW LIVING TRANSLATION

❧

JOY!

Jack Hayford

FROM *COME AND BEHOLD HIM*

A crystal punch bowl sparkles in the candlelight...
Tree lights reflect a spectrum on the windowpane...
Visions of sugarplums dance in children's dreams...
Joy!
A spontaneous embrace is filled with
grateful affection...
The warmth of a relationship is renewed
by a simple greeting card...
Mom and Dad share a deep closeness as they watch
their children playing with new toys...
Joy!
Potpourri fills the house with the
scent of the season...
Cider tingles on the tongues of carolers just
finishing their rounds...
Loved ones, filled with lazy satisfaction following the
holiday dinner, surround the hearth...
Joy!
And most joyous of all...He is with us.

A CHRISTMAS TRADITION

Shirley Dobson

FROM *LET'S MAKE A MEMORY*

These happy days of Christmas come and go so quickly that we have sought a way to hold on to the pleasure a while longer. Therefore, we have developed a custom of saving our Christmas cards from friends and loved ones far and wide, and after New Year's Day, I put them on a tray near the dinner table. Every night we select some cards and read them, along with the letters enclosed with them. We then pray for those families around our table. This tradition may take months to complete, depending on the number of cards we receive. With the busy days of Christmas behind us, we can better enjoy the beauty of the cards and absorb the meaningful verses and personal notes.

The Christmas traditions that we have developed through the years are not unique to the Dobson household. Perhaps yours are similar in many respects. But they are extremely meaningful to each member of our family. These activities serve to emphasize the two vitally important themes that embody the Christmas spirit: celebration of Jesus' birth and life, and celebration of love for one another and for the entire human family. As such, this exciting time of the year brings out the very best that is within us.

GOD REST YOU MERRY

"God rest you merry,

gentlemen..."

and in these pressured days

I, too, would seek to be so blessed

by Him, who still conveys

His merriment, along with rest.

So I would beg, on tired knees,

"God rest me merry,

please..."

Ruth Bell Graham

FROM *LEGACY OF A PACK RAT*

THE TREE
Crystal J. Kirgiss

Whether short or tall,
bent or straight,
young or old,
full or bare,
once chosen and decorated
with tender care
each tree becomes lovely,
bathed in lights,
wrapped in color,
clothed in newness...
a symbol of bent, bare empty lives
chosen by the Father,
bathed in Light,
wrapped in Hope,
clothed in Forgiveness,
REBORN,
because long ago
a tiny babe
entered our world
and shattered the darkness.

KEEPING CHRISTMAS
Peter Marshall

FROM *LET'S KEEP CHRISTMAS*

In a world that seems not only to be changing, but even to be dissolving, there are some tens of millions of us who want Christmas to be the same...with the same old greeting "Merry Christmas" and no other.

We long for the abiding love among men of good will which the season brings...believing in this ancient miracle of Christmas with its softening, sweetening influence to tug at our heartstrings once again.

We want to hold on to the old customs and traditions because they strengthen our family ties, bind us to our friends, make us one with all mankind for whom the Child was born, and bring us back again to the God Who gave His only begotten Son, that "whosoever believeth in Him should not perish, but have everlasting life."

So we will not "spend" Christmas...nor "observe" Christmas.

We will "keep" Christmas—keep it as it is... in all the loveliness of its ancient traditions.

May we keep it in our hearts, that we may be kept in its hope.

ONE SOLITARY LIFE
Adapted from James Allen Francis

He was born in an obscure village, the child of a peasant woman. He grew up in another village. He worked in a carpenter shop until he was thirty, and then for three years he was an itinerant preacher.

He never wrote a book.

He never held an office.

He never owned a home.

He never had a family.

He never went to college.

He never traveled more than two hundred miles from the place where he was born.

He never did any of the things that usually accompany greatness.

He had no credentials but himself.

While he was still a young man, the tide of public opinion turned against him. His friends ran away. He was turned over to his enemies and went through the mockery of a trial. He was nailed to a cross between two thieves. While he was dying, his executioners gambled for the only piece of property he had on earth, and that was his coat. When he was dead, he was laid in a borrowed grave through the kindness of a friend.

Nearly twenty centuries have come and gone, and today he is still the central figure of the human race and the leader of mankind's progress.

I am far within the mark when I say that. . .

all the armies that have ever marched,

all the navies that have ever sailed,
all the parliaments that have ever sat,
and all the kings that have ever reigned,
all put together, have not affected the life of man upon this
    earth as much as that One Solitary Life.

A CHRISTMAS PRAYER
Robert Louis Stevenson

Loving Father, help us to remember the birth of Jesus, that we may share in the song of the angels, the gladness of the shepherds, and the worship of the wise men.

Close the door of hate and open the door of love all over the world.

Let kindness come with every gift and good desires with every greeting.

Deliver us from evil by the blessing which Christ brings, and teach us to be merry with clear hearts.

May the Christmas morning make us happy to be Thy children, and the Christmas evening bring us to our beds with grateful thoughts, forgiving and forgiven, for Jesus' sake. Amen!

ACKNOWLEDGMENTS

Notes and acknowledgments are listed by story title in the order they appear in each section of the book. For permission to reprint any of the stories, please contact the original source listed.

It is with deep sincerity that I express my thankfulness to the authors and publishers who granted permission to have their stories included.

CHRISTMAS TREASURES

"The Manger Was Empty" retold by Casandra Lindell. Original author and source unknown. Used by permission of Casandra Lindell.

"Trouble at the Inn" by Dina Donohue. Reprinted with permission from *Guideposts* magazine. Copyright © 1966 by Guideposts, Carmel, NY 10512.

"The Gold and Ivory Tablecloth" by Howard C. Schade. Reprinted with permission from the December 1954 *Reader's Digest*, © 1954 by the Reader's Digest Association, Inc.

"If You're Missing Baby Jesus, Call 7162" by Jean Gietzen. Adapted from *If You're Missing Baby Jesus*, © 1999. Used by permission of Multnomah Publishers, Inc., Sisters, OR. All rights retained.

"Hi There!" by Nancy Dahlberg. Used by permission of the Office of Communication, *The American Baptist*. All rights retained.

"A String of Blue Beads" by Fulton Oursler. © 1951 by the Reader's Digest Association. Used by permission of the estate of Fulton Oursler.

Lindstedt. Original author and source unknown. Used by permission of Dave Lindstedt.

"Frankincense and Myrrh" by Heywood Broun from *Pieces of Hate.*

"The Legend of the Poinsettia" retold by Alice Gray. Original author and source unknown.

"The Legend of the Christmas Rose" retold by Casandra Lindell. Original author and source unknown. Used by permission of Casandra Lindell.

CHRISTMAS REFLECTIONS

"The Arrival" by Max Lucado from *God Came Near* (Sisters, OR: Multnomah Publishers, Inc., © 1987). Used by permission.

"Daily Gifts" by Charles R. Swindoll from *The Finishing Touch* (Nashville, TN: Word Publishing, © 1994). All rights reserved.

"The Birthplace of the King" by William Barclay from *The Gospel of Matthew, Volume 1* (Edinburgh: The Saint Andrew Press, © 1975).

"One Small Candle" by Michael Passons, from the award-winning singing group Avalon. Used by permission of the author.

"Next Time It Will Be Different!" taken from *God with Us* by John F. MacArthur, Jr. © 1989 by John F. MacArthur, Jr. Used by permission of Zondervan Publishing House.

"Jesus, Who Is He?" by Tim LaHaye from *Jesus, Who Is He?* (Sisters, OR: Multnomah Publishers, Inc., © 1996). Used by permission.

"The Glory of Humility" by Philip Yancey from *The Jesus I Never Knew* (Grand Rapids, MI: Zondervan Publishing House, © 1995 by Philip Yancey). Used by permission of Zondervan Publishing House.

"The Angels Called It Good News" by Larry Libby from *Someone Awesome* (Sisters, OR: Multnomah Publishers, Inc., Gold 'n' Honey Books, © 1995). Used by permission.

ACKNOWLEDGMENTS

ALL SONGS USED BY PERMISSION
ALL RIGHTS RESERVED

Christmas Is All In The Heart ~ Steven Curtis Chapman
From the Sparrow Records release, **The Music Of Christmas**
Produced by Brown Bannister for RBI Productions, Inc. and Steven Curtis Chapman
Written by Steven Curtis Chapman / ©1995 Sparrow Song / Peach Hill Songs / BMI /
Admin. by EMI Christian Music Publishing

Christmas Star ~ CeCe Winans
From the Pioneer Music Group/Sparrow Records release, **His Gift**
Produced by Steve Harvey / Written by Kevin Savigar & Kimmie Rhodes
©1998 Almo Music / Kevin Savigar Music / ASCAP /
Irving Music / Gracey Rhodes Music / BMI

Don't Save It All For Christmas Day ~ Avalon
From the upcoming Sparrow Records September 2000 release, **Joy**
Produced by Brown Bannister / Written by Peter Zizzo, Ric Wake & Celine Dion
©1998 WB Music Corp. / Make It Rock / Annotation Music / ASCAP /
Warner-Tamerlane Publishing / Connotation Music / Pez Music / BMI / Sony / ATV Songs / ASCAP

What Child Is This ~ Cheri Keaggy
From the Sparrow Records release, **God With Us**
Produced by Charlie Peacock / Arranged by Tim Akers & Charlie Peacock
Arr. ©1997 Rolling Akers Music / ASCAP / Sparrow Song
(admin. by EMI Christian Music Publishing) / Andi Beat Goes On Music
(admin. by EMI Christian Music Publishing) / BMI

The First Noel ~ Steve Green
From the Sparrow Records release, **The First Noel**
Produced by Phil Naish for NT Productions / Arranged by Phil Naish
Arr. ©1996 His Eye Music / SESAC / Admin. by EMI Christian Music Publishing

O Come, O Come Emmanuel ~ Margaret Becker
From the Sparrow Records release, **Christmas**
Produced by Billy Smiley / Arranged by Margaret Becker & Billy Smiley
Arr. ©1988 Birdwing Music / ASCAP / His Eye Music / SESAC /
Admin. by EMI Christian Music Publishing

O Holy Night ~ Out of the Grey
From the Sparrow Records release, **God With Us**
Produced by Charlie Peacock / Arranged by Pat Coil & Charlie Peacock
Arr. © i997 Recoil Music / Sparrow Song (admin. by EMI Christian Music Publishing) /
Andi Beat Goes On Music (admin. by EMI Christian Music Publishing) / BMI

The Kid In Me ~ Phillips, Craig & Dean
From the Star Song Records release, **Repeat The Sounding Joy**
Produced by Paul Mills for PCM Productions / Written by Dan Dean, Dave Clark &
Don Koch / ©1996 Dawn Treader Music (admin. by EMI Christian Music Publishing) /
SESAC / Word Music / First Verse Music / ASCAP / DaySpring Music / BMI

It's The Thought ~ Twila Paris
From the Star Song Records release, **It's The Thought**
Produced by Jonathan David Brown / Written by Twila Paris / ©1989 Ariose Music /
Mountain Spring Music / ASCAP / Admin. by EMI Christian Music Publishing

A Cradle Prayer ~ Rebecca St. James
From the ForeFront Records release, **Christmas**
Produced by Tedd T. / Written by Rebecca St. James & Charles Garrett
©1997 Sci-Phi Music Publishing (admin. by EMI Christian Music Publishing) / Songs On
The ForeFront (admin. by EMI Christian Music Publishing) / SESAC / Up In The Mix Music
(admin. by EMI Christian Music Publishing) / Bibbetsong Music / BMI